# Saxe's New Guide

*Hints to Soda Water Dispensers*

*by*

De Forest W. Saxe

APPLEWOOD BOOKS
*Bedford, Massachusetts*

*Saxe's New Guide*

was originally published in

1894

ISBN: 978-1-4290-1048-1

Thank you for purchasing an Applewood book.
Applewood reprints America's lively classics—
books from the past that are still of interest
to the modern reader.
For a free copy of
a catalog of our
bestselling
books,
write
to us at:
Applewood Books
Box 365
Bedford, MA 01730
or visit us on the web at:
For cookbooks: foodsville.com
For our complete catalog: awb.com

**Prepared for publishing by HP**

Include in your next order for our goods, a case or so of

# SAXE'S PHOSPHO=GUARANA

### WITH CELERY

A Most Popular Drink at the Soda Fount and the Finest

## NERVE TONIC

### IN EXISTENCE

*As a Thirst-Quencher it has no Equal*

| SPEEDY RELIEF | THE GREATEST |
| FOR | THIRST-QUENCHER |
| NERVOUS | IN |
| HEADACHE | THE WORLD |

## PHOSPHO=GUARANA FOR HOME USE

Put up in Quart Bottles, packed one dozen in a case; price, $6 per dozen, $72 per gross. It is very fine mixed with Ice Water. Retail price, $1 a Bottle; twenty-five drinks in each bottle.

"P. G." is a great seller and will increase your sales at the Fountain 50 per cent at least. Nervous people will come like clock work three (3) times a day for their drink, when they once learn its value.

MANUFACTURED BY

## BEACH & CLARRIDGE

### 52 TO 58 EASTERN AVENUE, - BOSTON, MASS.

AND

### THE VICTOR BAROTHY BOTTLERS SUPPLY CO.

409 Dearborn Street, CHICAGO.

LIBRARY
UNIVERSITY OF CALIFORNIA
DAVIS

## IMPORTANT.

I would call the attention of the dispensers who propose using or trying my formulas to the fact that the vital points, and the ones to be looked after first, will be found in

No. 13   How to draw a glass of soda.
No. 16   In regard to serving still drinks.
No. 21   About using shaved ice in soda.
No. 26   About the lining of portable fountains.
No. 27   List of drinks.
No. 28   The base of all flavored syrups.
No. 29   Simple syrup.
No. 30   Gum foam, best in the world.
No. 31   Fruit acid.
No. 32   The art of mixing.
No. 101   Egg drinks, and how made correctly.

Unless the instructions, as given in above numbers, are carried out in the start, my book will be of no use to you. It is the little points, which seem insignificant at first, that are essential to the success and reputation of a soda dispenser.

# DRINKS, WHICH IF PROPERLY SERVED AND PUSHED WILL MAKE YOU BOTH MONEY AND REPUTATION.

### STILL DRINKS
(For Quenching Thirst.)

### SAXE'S BLOOD ORANGE PHOSPHATE
(The finest in America.)

### RASPBERRY CORDIAL
(Made from my Formula is sure to draw and hold trade.)

### GINGER FRUIT
(Very cooling and refreshing.)

### KLUB SODA
(Popular with the men.)

### SAXE'S PHOSPHO-GUARANA
(Great nerve and brain tonic, also speedy relief for nervous headache.)

### BELFAST GINGER ALE
(Perfect.)

### THE GREAT VITALIZERS.

| | | | |
|---|---|---|---|
| Egg Flipp | Egg Calisaya | Egg Nog | Egg Phosphate |
| Egg Lemonade | Boston Flip | Golden Ade | Silver Ade. |

| | | | |
|---|---|---|---|
| Mint Freeze | Razzle Dazzle | Pine-apple Smash | Pineapple Glacé |
| Floating Island | Cream Shake | Almond Sponge | Flowing Stream. |

The above are extra fine drinks when made and served properly, but are not by any means the only good formulas in the book.

---

"Soda" Water Apparatus and Machinery.
New and Second-Hand.
Bargains in Fountains, Copper and Steel Oils, Essences and Colorings.
Repairs made promptly.

**THE VICTOR BAROTHY BOTTLERS SUPPLY CO.**
409 Dearborn Street, Chicago.

# SAXE'S NEW GUIDE,

— OR —

# HINTS TO SODA WATER DISPENSERS.

### COMPLETE AND MODERN

## FORMULÆ

FOR THE MANUFACTURE AND DISPENSING OF ALL CARBONATED DRINKS, CONTAINING FULL AND EXPLICIT DIRECTIONS FOR MAKING ALL THE LEADING POPULAR DRINKS OF THE AGE, AND GIVING MY

### Private Formulæ for Fancy Syrups and Fancy Mixed Drinks,

CONTAINING VALUABLE INFORMATION ON ALL SUBJECTS CONNECTED WITH THE SODA BUSINESS, WHICH WAS OBTAINED BY ACTUAL EXPERIMENT AND LONG STUDY, COVERING A PERIOD OF SEVENTEEN YEARS, TWO OR THREE OF THE FORMULÆ CONTAINED IN THIS WORK ALONE BEING WORTH TO THE DISPENSER DOUBLE THE COST OF THE BOOK.

### PRICE, $3.00,

THIRD EDITION.

BY

## D. W. SAXE.

CHICAGO:
THE SAXE GUIDE PUBLISHING CO., PUBLISHERS.
1894.

LIBRARY
UNIVERSITY OF CALIFORNIA
DAVIS

Entered according to act of Congress in the year 1890, by
DEFOREST W. SAXE,
In the Office of the Libarian of Congress.—All rights reserved.

W. P. DUNN CO., PRINTERS,
CHICAGO.

# TO DISPENSERS USING SAXE'S GUIDE.

For the benefit of our patrons, and especially those who are apt to think that a work of this kind is simply an *Advertising Scheme* to push some special make of Juices and Extracts, we would say: This book is gotten up especially for the *benefit* of our *patrons*, and we have been extremely careful not to use its pages to advance the sale of any one make of goods over another.

In a very few *formulas* we are obliged to specify whose *Extracts* to use simply because no one else makes the goods to produce the results, and we do it, *not* to help the manufacturer, but to save our customers the trouble and time in writing us for information in regard to the matter. Such formulas are rare in this work, and whenever our patrons feel that they do not care to order the goods to make these drinks, they can leave them off their list and still have more first-class formulas than they can use in one season. We specify *no* special *brand* of *Fruit Juices*, but advise our customers to be exceedingly careful to buy the best in the market or make their *own*.

**THE SAXE GUIDE PUBLISHING CO.**

# SAXE'S NEW GUIDE,

OR

## Hints to Soda Water Dispensers.

THIRD EDITION.

## INTRODUCTORY.

In compiling this book of formulas (which is my second edition, the first having been published in 1890), it is my aim to not only give, in as concise form as possible, all my practical working receipts for making syrups and fancy mixed drinks, but also all the latest and best formulas I have created, as well as those obtained from outside sources, which are popular with the trade, not only here in Chicago, but elsewhere. I have obtained the formulas for making a few of the popular drinks contained in this book, from some of our most eminent dispensers of the "cooling draught;" but the greater part of them are of my own creation, based upon long and careful study and practical experiment, covering a period of over seventeen years, to produce, at the lowest possible cost, the best results.

I have tried as far as possible to overcome the obstacles usually found in the ordinary formulas for making syrups, where the author is apt to have lost sight either of the cost of the finished syrup or the unnecessary time and trouble required in manipulating same.

The best proof I can offer of the superior quality of the syrups made from the enclosed formulas is that they are in use now at my own fountains and that customers will walk four or five blocks out of their way and past other fountains to get a drink of my soda.

On the following pages I give a short sketch of my experience in the manufacture and sale of carbonated drinks covering a period of seventeen years, giving information in regard to charging fountains, how to make the best carbonated waters, and showing the saving in cost to the dispenser. I do this simply to show parties who have fountains and who are skeptical in regard to the profit derived in the sale of carbonated drinks, that if properly attended to and carefully managed, they can make their soda business a feature of no small importance and besides draw other trade, which they probably never would get without the aid of the soda fountain.

If this little "work" should fall into the hands of some druggists and dispensers of soda water (as I have no doubt it will) who have had a similar experience, and are familiar with the facts contained in the following pages of "My Experience," I trust they will pass on without comment to the formulas, and it may be possible that they will find at least a few which are new to them, and which, if given a fair trial, will prove of some benefit. At any rate the book can do them no harm, and as it is published more for the benefit of the dispenser who has never had a chance to thoroughly study the inside workings of the soda business, I shall be content if it reaches the latter class and is of any benefit to them.

With best wishes to all dispensers who may have the fortune, or misfortune, to read my book, I am,

    Very truly yours,
    D. W. SAXE, *the Author*.
Published by the Saxe Guide Pub. Co.
    Chicago, Ill.

## THE AUTHOR'S EXPERIENCE.

In the fall of 1879 I purchased the bankrupt stock of drugs in the old "Snowden Drug Store," corner of Thirteenth and Farnam streets, Omaha, Neb. I paid for the same fifty cents on the dollar, which was all, if not more, than it was worth, as the stock had been invoiced high, and on account of the store having been closed for about three months previous to my purchase, I could not, of course, depend on much of my predecessor's trade. After paying for the stock and taking possession of the store, I found that I had very little cash left and, being almost a stranger in Omaha and quite young (barely twenty-one) for such an undertaking, I found it rather difficult to establish my credit on the start. That fall and the following winter were "hard times" for me, and in the spring, although I had tried every way imaginable to keep expenses as low as possible, I found I was slowly running behind hand, and unless I made some lucky move soon, I could not hold out long.

I had spent about five years in the drug business in the East, previous to my coming to Omaha, and had always taken great pride and interest in making the best soda water in the town where I was located, and while there had always enjoyed the cream of the trade in that line.

At the time I started in business in Omaha the population of the city was estimated at 21,000. I found on investigation that the druggists generally up to that time had paid very little attention to the sale of soda water and, in consequence, sold very little, even in the hottest weather. I found one exception to the rule, however, and that was in the person of John W. Bell, the genial and courteous druggist on Tenth street, near the U. P. Depot. He seemed to realize the fact that it paid to make good soda, and to give that part of his business as much of his personal time and attention as he could spare from his other duties. In consequence he had a very nice soda trade and without doubt made by far the finest carbonated drinks in the city.

After thinking the matter over for some time, I came to the conclusion that if my friend Bell, located as he was at that time away several blocks from the business part of the city, could capture all, or nearly all, of the soda trade by simply making better drinks than any one else in the business, I would see what I could do in a much better location. Accordingly on the 21st of April, 1880, I opened up the little fountain in my store, which I had purchased with other "traps" in the Snowden bankrupt stock. The apparatus was a small one with one soda draught tube, two minerals, and eight syrup cans, holding one-half gallon each, capacity for cooling about fifty pounds of ice; apparatus, I believe, cost originally $300.

I took particular pains my first season to serve good soda, and gave the business my personal attention, as I have always done, when not otherwise engaged, and although that summer was rather cool, and on account of it being my first season in the business, it took some time to establish a reputation. Still I sold between the months of April and October $1,094.80 worth of soda, which was about $700.00 more than had ever been sold in the store by my predecessor. I kept a separate book for my soda sales, and expense of running fountain, and the expense for that season including soda, boy, ice, syrups, cream, breakage and all other expense of running fountain amounted to $545.12, leaving me a net profit of $549.68, a little over 100 per cent. profit.

This encouraged me, and I determined to make a still greater effort the next season and see if I couldn't double my sales. I opened my

Saxe's Large Canopy Top Apparatus. 30 feet long, with 35 foot Counter.

fountain the following season, 1881, April 26th, and closed October 11th. It turned out to be an exceedingly warm summer, and with a little advertising in the way of an illuminated sign in my window and one outside in front of the store, and a thousand or so quarter sheet posters stuck up on the bill boards around town, I succeeded in surpassing my most sanguine expectations; selling that season $2,786.05; expense of selling same $1,325.10, leaving a net profit of $1,460.95. We had no water-works in Omaha at that time, and all the water used for rinsing tumblers and cleaning fountain had to be carried two blocks in pails. So when we stop to consider the amount of labor required under the circumstances, with a very small fountain and limited room for working, selling soda, as we were, at 5 cents a glass, nearly $2,800 in one season at that time was a big soda business.

In the fall of 1881 I rented the corner store under Boyd's Opera House, Fifteenth and Farnam, two blocks west of my old location, and, as I was fitting up the new store in nice shape, I decided to buy a new fountain and made arrangements for more room and better facilities for my fast increasing soda business. In the spring I put in a good sized counter apparatus and, as I had plenty of room for manufacturing the carbonated waters, I decided also to buy a generator. Up to this time I had always had my fountains charged at the bottling works, paying 12½ cents per gallon for same. After studying up the matter thoroughly, I made up my mind I could save from 25 to 50 per cent, by charging my own fountains. So I purchased with my new apparatus a *small Generator*, and began doing my own generating. That season was a bad one, being cold and rainy most of the time during the best three months of the season, May, June and July, consequently my soda trade suffered and the sales were less than the year before, amounting only to $2,626.00. but the expense was much less (on account of our charging our own founts), being only $1,063.91, which left a clean profit of $1,562.09. Showing that while the sales were short nearly $200.00 from the year previous, yet the profit was over $100.00 more.

### NO. 2.

In the winter of 1887, on account of my fast increasing soda trade, and a desire to know just what could be done in that line, with better facilities and more show, I bought a 15-foot Canopy Top Apparatus, one of the first ever introduced in the West. I spent considerable time in having this apparatus arranged for convenience, and in getting up new drinks to open with, and I also secured the services of a first-class soda expert, to open with. Up to this time we had never drawn cold soda in the winter, and my largest soda sales for the season just past were about $4,000. I opened my new apparatus on February 1st, with a list of cold drinks numbering about 125, and also a few hot drinks. The new apparatus, new drinks, and soda men in white coats and aprons, proved a drawing card, and during the twenty-eight days of that month my soda sales amounted to $1,410, or an average of about $50 a day, and for the year, from February 1, 1887, to February 1, 1888, a little over $8,000, or just about double what I had ever sold in any preceding year. During the following three years, 1888, '89 and '90, I sold $44,950 worth of soda, or an average of about $15,000 a year.

### NO. 3.

Many people claim that a small, neat apparatus, with good attendance and good drinks, is all that is necessary, and that it does not pay to have so much cash tied up in a large apparatus. My experience has been that it is best to keep up with the times in the soda business, as well as in other branches of trade, and while one may be able to draw a good glass of soda from an old-fashioned apparatus, still people like to drink at a fine, elegant fountain best, provided the drinks and service are first-class.

The great mistake nine-tenths of the druggists and confectioners make is in buying a large, fine apparatus, and then expecting it to run itself, never changing the drinks, or trying to introduce anything new or novel. This won't do, for the trade naturally expect new drinks and better service with a new apparatus. I do not mean by new drinks that it is necessary to buy every patent drink on the market, but get them up yourself, and save the manufacturers and jobbers' profit. You will find by figuring on the cost of my formulas, as given in this book, that the average cost of the finished syrups is from 45 to 55 cents per gallon, figuring granulated sugar at 5 cents per pound.

## NO. 4.

It is not necessary to make all the drinks given in this book to start with, but select from the list forty or fifty of the best formulas and make them up, and then, every week or so, bring forward a new drink and advertise it a little. By experiment you can soon tell which drinks suit your trade best, and then it will pay to push them for all they are worth, making " leaders " of a few of the most popular ones.

### NO. 5.

I have given the exact figures in regard to my soda trade from year to year, simply to show to what extent the soda business can be worked up to if the dispenser will only give it the time and attention he does his other business. Competition is becoming so close in the drug business, and prices are being cut so on all patents, and on sundries, that the druggist stands little or no show of making any money without some specialty. So why not make a specialty of soda water, as it is in our line and nearly every body has invested in a soda fountain from one-eighth to one-fourth of his entire capital.

I sold out my business in 1891, in Omaha, and came to Chicago, for the purpose of pushing my Guide, and also because the field is larger for the soda business generally. During the summer of 1892, I had several soda stands in different parts of Chicago, and did a thriving business.

When I first opened my apparatus in Chicago, (in my principal place) I put in two of my old experts who had been with me in Omaha, and who had learned (under my instruction) my way of serving drinks, and of catering to the taste of the people. We put on the same list of drinks that we had in Omaha, adding a few new leaders, (which are all given in this work, as well as the old reliable ones) and in a very short time we had the finest trade in Chicago coming to our place for drinks. Many came at first just to see my men mix drinks, but they soon found out that I not only had the best dispensers in the city, but also the most delicious drinks in the country.

This stand is located at the N. W. cor. of State and Randolph sts., a little out of the way for transient, and yet we have a regular trade now that will walk two or three blocks out of their way to get our soda. It has been a soda stand for years, but very little soda had been sold there till I took possession, simply because it had not been properly pushed.

One drink alone I will mention here as having helped very materially to build up my trade and establish our reputation in Chicago, and that is Saxe's Blood Orange Phosphate, a simple drink, quickly served, and as quickly drank, and affording a larger per cent of profit at five cents a glass, than ice cream soda at ten cents. I have never yet seen an Orange Phosphate that would hold the trade, and bring people out of their way to drink, like my own, and it is a very hard drink to copy, unless you have the formula for making it.

I paid $25.00 for this receipt in Boston several years ago, and it has been worth ten times its cost to me. It is especially valuable to a dispenser who is doing a large soda trade in a limited space, for the reason that it can be served so quickly, and customers waste no time in drinking it, thus making room for others, while the nickels accumulate in the cash drawer much faster than when serving ice cream soda, which takes so long to serve, and also to drink.

My advice is, educate your trade to drink something else besides ice cream soda, unless you want to make an ice cream parlor of your store.

On the following pages you will find a few instructions in regard to running a generator and how to make your carbonated waters clear and sparkling, giving cost of same as compared with that purchased from the bottling works. After that comes my formulas for making syrups and fancy drinks, comprising a list of about 175, some of which are my choicest formulas, and for which I have been offered from $25 to $50. I give them all in this work, including such new drinks as I consider worth mentioning, and trust that whoever tries them may meet with as good success as I have done.

Asking the reader's pardon for having made my "Experience" so long, I will close.

THE AUTHOR.

## NO. 6.

### HOW TO MAKE THE BEST CARBONATED WATER AT THE LOWEST POSSIBLE COST.

Each manufacturer of generators furnishes a book giving full directions in regard to charging fountains, and explaining how carbonic acid gas is obtained by the action of the acid on either marble dust or soda, thus liberating the carbonic acid in a gaseous form.

## NO. 7.

Tuft's formula for charging 30 gallons water at a pressure of 150 pounds with the No. 3 Sterling generator is:

| | | |
|---|---|---|
| Bi-Carbonate Soda | 17 | lbs. |
| Oil Vitriol | 3 | qts. |
| Water in Alkali Chamber | 2½ | " |
| Water in Purifier | 2 | " |
| Cost, not including labor. | | $1.02 |

## NO. 8.

I have found by actual experiment that I can do better. By using a little more material I can charge 60 to 65 gallons of water at the same pressure.

My formula for 60 gallons is:
  Bi-Carbonate Soda "*Natrona.*" 22  lbs.
  Oil Vitriol . . . . . . 3½  qts.
  Water in Purifier . . . . 2   "
  Water in Alkali Chamber . 3   "
   Cost, not including labor .    $1.30

### NO. 9.

*It pays to charge your own founts*, especially if you are doing business in a town where there is no bottling works and are obliged to ship by freight to some larger town to have them charged. The freight on founts alone costing you as much as the soda.

### NO. 10.

#### CHARGING FOUNTS.

In charging founts great care should be exercised in using pure filtered water free from all organic matter and as cold as possible.

As it is almost impossible to get pure water, free from organic matter, it is best in all cases to use a filter, for then you know you are all right, and as pure water is absolutely necessary and essential in producing first-class soda and mineral water, it is well to give this matter close attention, and be sure you have a good filter.

The Derham Patent Verhage Filter, made of solid stone about three inches in thickness through which the water passes, is in my judgment one of the most practical and economical filters in use at the present time; simple in construction, easily cleaned and moderate in price and will filter the muddiest water without the use of alum.

In filling my founts I have a large tin funnel holding about one and one-half gallons with a piece of wire strainer soldered across the inside about three inches from the bottom, supported by heavy iron wire also soldered across just under the strainer and also above. I then fill the funnel nearly full of cracked ice, through which I pour my filtered water. What are called 10 gallon fountains hold about 14 gallons and the smaller ones in proportion, room being left for agitating the carbonated water. To draw a nice glass of soda, providing the syrups are good, it is very essential that the fountains should be well shaken while being charged. When your gauge shows that you have about 180 pounds pressure on, let the gas over into the fountain slowly, agitating the same all the time by means of a wooden rocker. The first time when all the gas has gone from generator to fountain that can, your gauge will show that you have probably about 75 pounds pressure in the fountain; turn off the gas valve on top of purifier, let down more acid in the alkali chamber and run up the pressure again to 180 pounds, shaking fountain thoroughly all the time. You will find if fount is thoroughly shaken, that when you let over the gas a second time, after all has gone over that can, you still have only about 75 to 80 pounds pressure, showing that a large per cent. of the gas has been absorbed by the water. Repeat the operation several times until gauge shows a second time a pressure of 150 pounds, then detach fountain from generator, and continue as before with the second fount. After founts are charged keep them in cellar if possible, or in some cool place. When through charging always clean your generator at once; and leave both the acid and alkali chambers about half full of water until you are ready to charge again.

## NO. 11.

### LIQUEFIED GAS.

Since coming to Chicago I have tried the liquefied gas for charging, and I find it works very nicely. In fact, it is so much more convenient, and such a saving of labor, I have discontinued the use of my generator altogether. The cost is just about the same as when using a generator, if you figure the time and labor as anything, and as the machine takes up so little room, and is so clean, and easy to charge with, it is no wonder that the liquid gas is becoming so popular. One great advantage it has over a generator, and that is, that the gas in passing from a liquid to a gaseous state becomes very cold, and chills the water without having to use ice, which improves the quality of the carbonated water very materially.

## NO. 12.

### KEEP YOUR APPARATUS CLEAN AND ATTRACTIVE.

Nothing adds more to the reputation of the dispenser than the fact that his fountain is always kept neat and clean, with a clean dispensing counter, clean glasses, and a clean boy with clean hands in attendance.

If your business will warrant you keeping a boy, or man, all the time at the fountain, by all means have him wear a clean white coat and apron, and require him to keep his hands clean. Ladies will notice and appreciate all these little things and it will advertise your business.

### NO. 13.

### HOW TO DRAW A GLASS OF SODA.

Never allow a green hand to draw a glass of soda for a lady, let him practice first on himself and then on the small boy customer. Almost as much depends on the way a glass of soda is drawn as on the syrups and carbonated water. Always give your customers a good solid glass of soda, with a liberal allowance of cream, topping off the glass with a fine creamy foam. Never ask customers if they will have cream, for half of them don't know whether or not they want it. Give them cream anyway, unless they request you not to, for as a rule it adds 50 per cent. to the quality of the drink. Even at 5 cents a glass you can well afford to give good cream and draw a solid drink. I am speaking of the old reliable flavors, of course, and of Sweet Cream. Not Ice Cream.

### NO. 14.

### HOW TO DRAW A GLASS OF ICE CREAM SODA.

Very few dispensers know how to draw a glass of ice cream soda properly. This may seem strange, but nevertheless it is a fact. The usual method is syrup first, ice cream next, then a little wind and water, that's all. This makes a very unsatisfactory drink, as it is not properly mixed, and *cannot* be properly mixed when served in this manner, unless you use a spoon and make mush of it. In drinking a glass of soda served as above, 1st you taste wind, 2d plain soda, 3d ice cream, 4th syrup, all separate. This leads the customer to think that your ice cream soda is bad, and he goes out dissatisfied, but had you mixed the drink properly, using the same material, no doubt he would have been well pleased.

I always teach my soda men to draw the syrup first, then turn on the fine soda stream a moment, then the coarse, and again the fine till the glass is about one-half full, and the syrup is thoroughly mixed with the water, then drop in the ice cream, and top off with the fine stream of soda. In this way you have a glass of soda thoroughly mixed, with the ice cream in the center, floating around, and not adhering to the sides of the glass. Try my way and see if your customers are not better satisfied with the result.

### NO. 15.

#### STILL DRINKS.

In drawing what are called "Still Drinks" we never use cream. As a rule give ladies and children more syrup than you do men.

## NO. 16.

### STILL DRINKS.

These drinks are made by drawing an ordinary eight-ounce mineral glass seven-eighths full of plain soda and then adding the syrup, and generally a little acid phosphate, stirring with a spoon.

## NO. 17.

### ALCOHOL IN SODA.

If you have two draught tubes and separate coolers for same, so you can have two fountains attached all the time, add to each 14-gallon fountain of soda you intend to use for your "foam" drinks, 2 ounces of alcohol or 2 teaspoonfuls of bi-carbonate of soda (I prefer the alcohol), but for your still drinks use the plain carbonated water.

## NO. 18.

### TO DRAW A SOLID DRINK.

In drawing a glass of soda, when you put in the syrup first, you will find you can draw a good solid glassful much quicker by using the fountain that contains the alcohol, while for still drinks it is just the reverse.

### NO. 19.
### LOOK OUT FOR YOUR CREAM CAN.

Scald out your cream can every time before putting in fresh cream, and occasionally use a little sal-soda in your hot water. *Never* mix new cream with the old, and *never* substitute condensed milk for the cream, unless you want your soda trade to die an unnatural death.

Some of the manufacturers of soda water apparatus recommend the use of "condensed milk" where pure cream is scarce or high, but I would sooner pay $2. per gallon for the genuine, or else use none at all, rather than substitute so inferior an article.

---

### NO. 20.

### HOW TO AVOID THE DELAY OF CHANGING FOUNTAINS IN A RUSH.

If your apparatus is small and you have only one draught tube for soda, purchase of any manufacturer of soda supplies what is called a "two (2) way cock" (cost about $2), attach same, under the counter, to soda pipe leading to cooler in the fount, and screw the plate which is attached to way cock tightly to side of counter. At the bottom it has two connections for soda pipes, which are attached to same and then to two fountains of soda. It has a lever or switch which can be turned either to the right or left, so when one fount of soda runs out, which generally happens in a rush, all you have to do is to turn the switch and in less time than one minute you can draw from the second fount. After the rush is over and you have time, you can detach the empty and replace with a full fount.

### NO. 21.

#### ABOUT USING SHAVED ICE IN SODA.

Many dispensers think it the correct thing to use shaved ice in soda, and accordingly go to the expense of buying a machine for that purpose, making the soda boy nearly grind his arm off in the desperate attempt to shave enough ice to keep up with the trade. This is entirely unnecessary and in fact is a detriment, as it detracts from, rather than adding to, the quality of the drink. It takes the life all out of the soda, leaving it flat and tasteless. I used an ice shave one or two seasons when they were in style; paid, I think, $100.00 for it and afterward sold it for $15.00.

If you are buying a new apparatus, pay particular attention to the coolers, and see that they are of the latest and most approved style, and you will need no ice shaver.

## NO. 22.

### HOW TO KEEP SODA COLD.

*In putting ice on the coolers* crush it vey fine for the first and second layers, and after that fill up with pieces about the size of a hen's egg or a little larger, covering same with a piece of heavy cloth or bagging, which will help to keep the ice from melting.

If the ice is packed closely around your pipes and coils, and the cooler is kept full all day, you ought not to have any complaints about your soda not being cold enough. Occasionally you will find a man who will complain and say your soda is warm, but ten chances to one he would complain if you put in shaved ice, complain of its being too cold.

---

## NO. 23.

Of course if your apparatus is quite small the cooling capacity must be limited, and in case you happen to have an unusual rush, or your trade is very large anyway, you may not be able to keep your soda as cool as it should be. In that case the only remedy I can suggest would be to buy a new apparatus to meet the demands of your trade. This is the rule I have always followed.

As my trade increases from year to year and I find my fountain too small to do the work required of it, I sell the old and purchase a new one with greater capacity to meet the wants of my trade. Ten years ago when I purchased my second apparatus I thought it was large enough to accommodate my trade for at least the next ten years, but four years since I was obliged to throw it out and buy the third one. My new apparatus was made expressly for me, and was built according to my own ideas, to dispatch the greatest amount of work in the shortest possible time. It is one of the most practical fountains ever made. Capacity for ice about 700 pounds. Capacity for syrups sixty gallons, with four draught tubes for soda, and four for minerals. When properly filled and packed with ice, with four boys drawing soda at one time, the temperature of the soda is from 34 to 36 degrees above zero, and remains unchanged, even during our greatest rushes in the hottest weather. As 32 degrees is the freezing point, soda drawn at from 34 to 36 is cold enough for any one, and we never have any complaint.

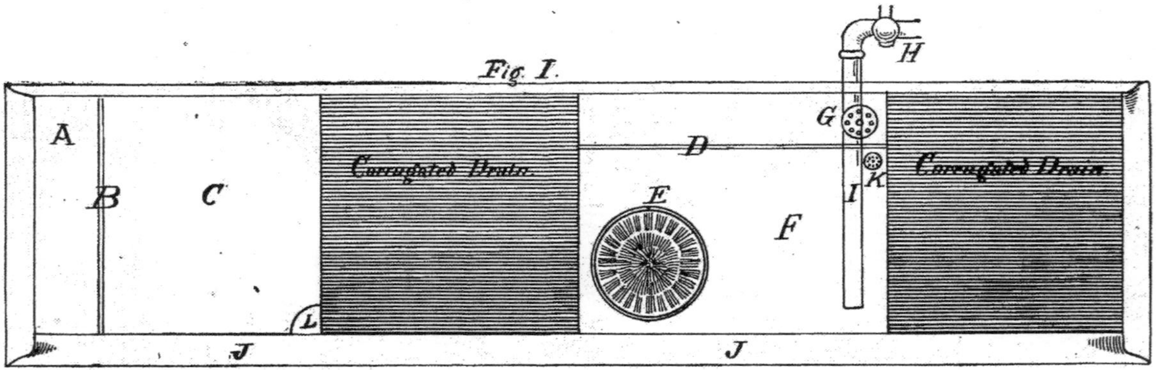


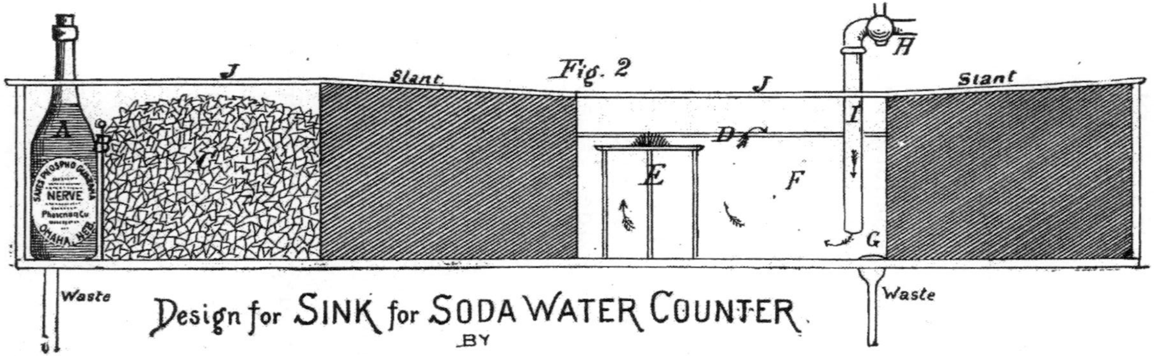


Design for SINK for SODA WATER COUNTER
BY
**D. W. SAXE**-ORIGINAL

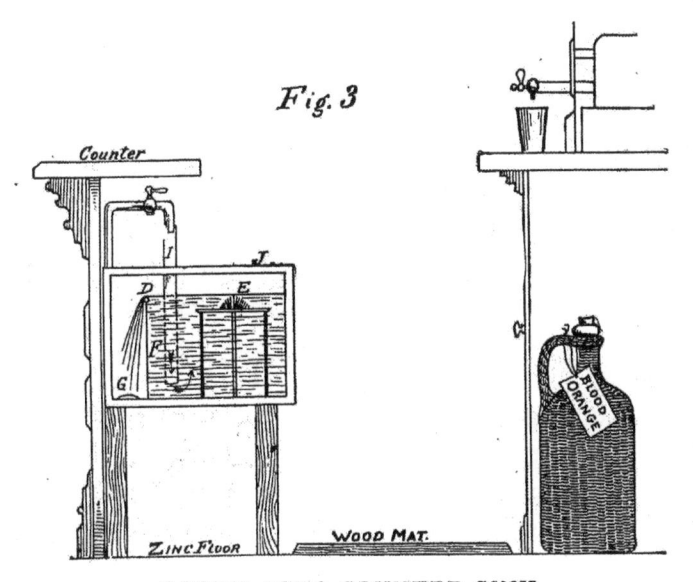

## SAXE'S SODA COUNTER SINK.

Fig. 1—Top view; Fig. 2—Side view; Fig. 3—End view.
Letters correspond for parts in each Fig.

A—Space for bottles next to fine chipped ice.
B—Sheet copper division—Top of division 2 inches below top of sink—Division perforated.
C—Space for two pails of chipped fine ice.
D—Dam for water to flow over into waste pipe.
E—Brush glass washer—Best for use.
F—Sink for clean flowing water.
G—Waste Pipe at bottom, back of dam
H—Hydrant.
I—Rubber pipe to conduct water to bottom which flows up into sink (see arrows) and over the dam. Carries away all dirt and slime.
J—Catch for water in front. Main waste pipe should be 4 inches in diameter (not less) with trap below the sink.
K—Waste pipe in sink connected from under side with waste G.
L—Partition in Ice box for throwing egg shells and lemon peel through into pail underneath.

## NO. 24.

### RUNNING WATER AT THE FOUNT.

If you are doing business in a town where there are water works and good sewerage put in a small sink under your dispensing counter about 12 inches deep with overflow about 8 inches from the bottom, and water faucet just over sink, as low as possible, so when turned on the water will not spatter; then have a corrugated drainer, made of copper or galvanized iron, with one end resting just over the edge of sink and slanting in that direction so it will drain itself. It is very hard to keep glasses clean without running water, and there is nothing that will drive away a customer quicker than serving your drinks in dirty glasses.

---

## NO. 25.

If flowers are plentiful and cheap, a nice bouquet of fresh cut flowers on your counter every morning will add to the appearance of the surroundings. In fact, any little thing which suggests itself to your mind that is pleasing to the eye and will beautify the appearance of the fountain and dispensing counter will help to draw trade.

### NO. 26.

**LOOK AFTER THE RE-LINING, OR RE-TINNING OF YOUR FOUNTAINS.**

It is very important that you should examine your copper or steel founts at least once each year, to see if they need re-lining, especially if they are tin-washed. After unscrewing the cap or head of fount you can easily ascertain, by means of a lighted candle attached to a piece of wire and inserted in the opening, whether or not the lining is in good condition. When you find dark spots of a greenish tint in the lining, you may know that it is unsafe to use the fount longer until it is thoroughly overhauled and re-lined.

Founts used for mineral water need attention much oftener than those used for plain soda. The salts act on the block tin much quicker than the carbonic acid does.

The action of the acid on the copper, after the lining is gone, forms *verdigris* which, as we all know, is not "conducive to good health" when taken "ad-libitum."

### NO. 27.

**LIST OF DRINKS.**

A good plan to avoid answering innumerable questions as to what drinks you serve, and the price of same, is to make out a complete list giving price of each drink, and have it printed in large type on a neat piece of heavy card board, which should be suspended directly over the dispensing counter in such a position that the customer can not help seeing and reading it.

### NO. 28.

**THE BASE OF NEARLY ALL FLAVORED SYRUPS.**

There are three important ingredients which should form the base of nearly all flavored syrups, they are :

Simple Syrup, Gum Foam and Fruit Acid.

### NO. 29.

**SIMPLE SYRUP.**

Best Granulated Sugar - - 6 lbs.
Pure Filtered Water, enough for 1 gal.

Make by the cold process of percolation, as syrup made cold will keep longer than if made by heat; or a very simple and convenient way of making it is to use a 10-gallon keg taking out the head. Into this put 30 pounds sugar and then add water till keg is half full, using a wooden paddle to stir with, the sugar will soon dissolve if stirred occasionally, leaving a clear, nice syrup. Strain before using.

## NO. 30.

### GUM FOAM.

| | |
|---|---|
| Soap Bark in Coarse Powder | 4 oz. |
| Glycerine | 4 " |
| Pure Water | 12 " |

Pack the soap bark firmly in a conical glass percolator, and add the glycerine and water, previously mixed, allowing same to macerate for two or three hours. Use a small amount of absorbent cotton in bottom of percolator, to allow the liquid to pass through, which will make it clear enough for use. To allow the mixture to macerate, insert a cork in small end of percolator, and cover top with anything suitable for the purpose. When it has stood long enough, pull out the cork and let the liquid pass through into a glass jar or bottle. It is then ready for use.

---

## NO. 31.

### FRUIT ACID.

| | |
|---|---|
| Citric Acid | 16 oz. |
| Filtered Water | 16 " |

Mix, and when acid is all dissolved run through cotton to free it from any particles of dirt which may be in the acid.

Fruit acid should always be used in all syrups made from fruit juices, to bring out the flavor of the fruit. For instance, in making Pine Apple, Strawberry, Raspberry, Orange, Cherry, etc., if you do not use a little fruit acid you will find your syrup when mixed with the carbonated water is flat and insipid and comparatively tasteless, and, while you may detect the flavor of the juice used, yet you will notice there is something lacking. By the addition of one-half ounce of fruit acid to the gallon of syrup you will readily notice the improvement it makes.

*Gum foam* is used to take the place of Cooper's Gelatine, or the white of eggs, for producing a nice creamy foam on soda that will last. It is an improvement on either of the latter, because it can be used in syrup made by the cold process, while gelatine or egg has to be added when the syrup is hot. You will notice my formulas for gum foam contain no alcohol, while others made for the same purpose do. Alcohol takes the life out of the *foam*, and as water and glycerine are sufficient to extract the principle required from the soap bark, it is unnecessary to use alcohol.

---

### NO. 32.

### THE ART OF MIXING.

The growth of the soda business during the past five years is simply wonderful, and it is fast becoming the principal part of the retailers' business, instead of a simple side issue. The time has passed (and very fortunately, too, for the customer) for a ten-year-old boy to draw soda, and it now requires, to do any business, a first-class man in every respect, one who has not only learned to make the syrups properly, but also, what is even of greater importance, one who knows how to mix and serve the drink in the most artistic style, proportioning the different flavors in such a way that they will not only tickle the palate and please the eye of the customer, but when drank will leave such a pleasant after-taste that the party drinking will surely call again.

I think I can safely say that nine-tenths of the proprietors of soda stands give much more attention to making fine syrups, and a big display of crushed fruits and *preserves* on their counters, than they do to the proper mixing of the drinks. I do not mean to say that too much care is observed in making pure, wholesome syrups, for one can not be too careful in that respect, but I do say that from close observation I find only occasionally (even at some of the finest soda stands in the country) soda men who are competent to mix drinks properly. The comparison between a good soda man and the ordinary run of them is about the same as that of a fine mixer at a high-toned bar and a common beer-slinger in a second rate saloon. Very few soda men who have worked for me (and I have had a great many of them in the past ten years) knew how to draw correctly even a plain glass of soda with sweet cream, at first, even though they had been in the business before, and some of them for years, and as for mixing fancy drinks to make them palatable, and to suit the taste of the customer, I have found very few who could do it properly.

It is the little points in mixing drinks that are most important, and are overlooked by the ordinary dispenser: for instance, such as too much ice in making an egg drink, pouring from glass to shaker and from shaker to glass too long, making the drink too dead and solid, or in other cases the reverse, making the drink all wind, which will not do. To mix properly requires not only good judgment, but practice under an experienced teacher. I have taken young men to work for me who never had drawn a glass of soda in their lives, and taught them in one season enough about the business so they were able the next to command good wages, and often more than men who had been drawing soda for years for some one else. In giving formulas for my fancy drinks, I have tried as best I could to explain just how they should be mixed, giving the exact proportion of each ingredient used, and telling also how to serve them, etc., etc. Any one with a fair knowledge of the soda business, and a desire to improve all the time, ought to be able, after studying carefully my formulas, to produce the same results as I do, and make as fine drinks as can be made.

# PLAIN AND FANCY SYRUPS.

### NO. 33.

#### AMBROSIA.

| | |
|---|---|
| Raspberry Syrup | 2 pts. |
| Vanilla Syrup | 2 " |
| Claret Wine (St. Julien) | 4 oz. |
| Gum Foam | 1 " |

Mix.

### NO. 34.

#### BANANA.

| | |
|---|---|
| Banana Extract | 1 oz. |
| Fruit Acid | ½ " |
| Simple Syrup | 1 gal. |
| Gum Foam | 1 oz. |

Mix.

### NO. 35.

#### CHOCOLATE NO 1.

Take one pound Baker's or Hance Bros. Powdered Soluble Chocolate, rub it thoroughly with a little hot water till a smooth, fine paste is formed, then add sufficient water to make the whole measure one gallon. Add twelve pounds granulated sugar and heat over a slow fire until dissolved. Strain through flannel, and when cold add one ounce *Ext. Vanilla.*

---

### NO. 36.

### "SAXE'S CHOCOLATE" NO. 2.

Put ¾ pound Baker's chocolate, whole, into 1 quart hot water, bring to a boil, allowing chocolate to dissolve without being powdered first, then boil till the mixture is quite thick, when it is allowed to cool, and while cooling rub carefully with a wooden spoon, or pestle, to make it smooth and even. Add enough syrup to make one gallon and allow to stand for two hours in an open vessel; you will then notice a greasy substance or scum which rises to the surface. This should be removed and after adding one-half ounce vanilla extract, you will have as nice a chocolate syrup as one could ask for, and besides, it will not separate like the ordinary chocolate syrup.

### NO. 37.
#### YABARA CHOCOLATE.
*Too Expensive for 5c Soda, but Very Fine.*

Take 3 pounds best sweet chocolate (vanilla flavor), add to 1 quart boiling water, when dissolved add 1 gallon pure cream, bring to a boil and then add 12 pounds granulated sugar. Stir with wooden spoon until thoroughly dissolved and mixed. Allow to cool, and then keep on ice, but not in syrup can, as it is too thick to draw nicely.

---

### NO. 38.
#### COFFEE SYRUP.

Take 1 pound best Mocha and Java coffee mixed, and ground rather coarse, put into a gallon percolator with a little absorbent cotton in bottom. Put 12 pounds granulated sugar in porcelain-lined kettle or pan, holding from two to three gallons, place same directly under percolator, then pour boiling water on to coffee and allow to percolate through on to sugar while hot, until enough has passed through to make two gallons syrup. Stir with wooden spoon until all is dissolved, then add two ounces gum foam, and it is ready for use. This makes the best coffee syrup I have ever used, and gives universal satisfaction.

### NO. 39.

#### RED CURRANT.

Red Currant Juice (A. H. Peloubet's) - - - - 10 oz.
Fruit Acid - - - - ¼ "
Gum Foam - - - - 1 "
Simple syrup, enough for - 1 gal.
Mix.

---

### NO. 40.

#### CANTON GINGER SYRUP.

Ginger Fruit Extract (B. & C.'s) 6 oz.
Fruit Acid - - - - 1 "
Simple Syrup - - - - 1 "
   Mix and draw still.

---

### NO. 41.

#### CRAB APPLE CIDER SYRUP.

Crab Apple Champagne (B.&C.'s) 7 oz.
Simple Syrup    add    1 gal.
   Mix and serve still.

## NO. 42.

### DIAMOND SYRUP.

| | |
|---|---|
| Vanilla Syrup | 1 pt. |
| Pineapple Syrup | 1 " |
| Lemon Syrup | 1 " |
| Honey, strained | 2 oz. |
| Fruit Acid | ⅛ " |
| Eggs, well beaten | 3 in number |
| Gum Foam | 3 teaspoonfuls. |
| Phospho Guarana Syrup | 1 pt. |

Mix.

This makes an excellent combination and a good seller.

---

## NO. 43.

### CREAM SYRUP.

| | |
|---|---|
| Fresh Cream | ½ pt. |
| Fresh Milk | ½ " |
| Powdered Sugar | 1 lb. |

Mix by shaking, and to keep from souring add a few grains bi-carbonate soda. Keep in a cool place.

## NO. 44.

### DON'T CARE SYRUP.

| | |
|---|---|
| **Good** Brandy | ½ pt. |
| Simple Syrup | 1 gal. |
| Gum Foam | 1 oz. |
| Fruit Acid | ¼ " |

Mix.

---

## NO. 45.

### GINGER SYRUP.

| | |
|---|---|
| Extract Jamaica Ginger | 1 oz. |
| (See formula below.) | |
| Fruit Acid | 3-8 oz. |
| Gum Foam | 1 oz. |
| Simple Syrup | 1 gal. |

Caramel enough to color.

Mix.

---

## NO. 46.

### EXTRACT JAMAICA GINGER—FOR GINGER SYRUP.

Jamaica Ginger in coarse powder 2 lbs.
Alcohol, pure - - - ½ gal.

Pack the ginger (dry) in a conical glass percolator with small piece of absorbent cotton at bottom. Pour on the alcohol and allow to pass through into a glass bottle. After all has gone through that will, pour on about 1 quart filtered water to drive out the remaining alcohol, and when the finished extract measures ½ gallon, remove the percolator and add to the extract enough caramel, if necessary, to give it a reddish brown color. It is then ready for use and is much better than when made from African ginger.

## NO. 47.

### GINGER ALE, "BELFAST."

Ginger Ale Extract (B. & C.) 6 oz.
Fruit Acid - - - 2 "
Simple Syrup, enough for 1 gal.

Mix, and use in the proportion of 1 ounce syrup to 7 ounces soda in mineral glass, drawing soda first and stirring with a spoon.

The B. & C. extract is made by Beach & Clarridge, of Boston, manufacturing chemists, and is by far the best I have ever used, making a drink so near like the imported *Belfast Ale* that it is hard to distinguish the difference. I have a large trade on this drink.

### NO. 48.

### GINGER FRUIT.

Ginger Fruit Extract - 6 oz.
Fruit Compound - - 10 "
Simple Syrup, enough for 1 gal.

Mix, and serve the same as ginger ale. All fancy syrups should be 10 cents a glass, though there is a good profit on them at 5 cents.

---

### NO. 49.

### GINGER FIZZ.

This drink is made the same as ginger fruit, only you add a small spoonful of powdered sugar, which makes the fizz.

---

### NO. 50.

### HOCK OR CLARET SYRUP.

Hock or Claret Wine - 1 pt.
Simple Syrup - - - 2 "
Gum Foam - - ½ oz.
  Mix.

## NO. 51.

### "HONEY DEW."

| | | |
|---|---|---|
| Brandy | - - | 2 oz. |
| Catawba Wine | - - | 4 " |
| Essence of Cloves | - | ½ " |
| Strawberry Juice | - - | 4 " |
| Blood Orange Extract | | ½ " |
| Pineapple Juice | - | 4 " |
| Essence Rose | - - | 1 " |
| Essence Mace | - | ¼ " |
| Gum Foam | - - | 2 " |
| Simple Syrup, enough for | | 2 gal. |

Mix.

---

## NO. 52.

### JAMAICA GINGER WINE.

| | | |
|---|---|---|
| Jamaica Ginger Wine | - | 2 oz. |
| Carbonated Water | - | 6 " |
| Acid Phosphate | - - | 1 teaspoonful |
| Powdered Sugar | - | 1 " |

Mix, and serve still.

---

## NO. 53.

### "KLUB SODA."

| | | |
|---|---|---|
| Klub Soda Extract | - | 2 oz. |
| Fruit Acid | - | 1 " |

Gum Foam -         - 1 "
Blood Orange Color   ½ teaspoonful
Simple Syrup, en'gh for 1 gal.
 Mix.

---

### NO. 54.

**SAXE'S BEST LEMON SYRUP.**

Oil of Lemon, best   -   28 drops
Citric Acid       -      1¼ ozs.
Simple Syrup      -      1 gal.
Tr. Curcuma enough to color.
Gum Foam       -         1 oz

Powder the citric acid in a mortar and add the oil of lemon, rub thoroughly till the oil is cut, then add syrup, gum foam and coloring. *Liebman & Butler's* best oil lemon will produce the finest flavor. It is very expensive, costing $9.00 per pound, but as it is warranted not to spoil, and as fifteen drops will give better results than twenty-eight (28) drops of any other oil in the market, I consider it the cheapest in the end. I have made lemon syrup from a number of different formulas but have never yet found one to equal the above, or that could be made for less money. Below I give a formula for making Tr. of Curcuma, which if carefully used will give the exact color lemon syrup should be. Only a few drops to the gallon are necessary.

## NO. 55.

### TR. CURCUMA.

Curcuma Root in powder - 3 oz.
Dilute Alcohol enough to make 1 pt.

Moisten the powder with 2½ ounces of dilute alcohol and macerate for 2 hours, then pack it firmly in a cylindrical percolator and gradually pour dilute alcohol upon it until two pints of tincture are obtained.

---

## NO. 56.

### LEMON SHERBET.

Lemon Syrup - 2 pts.
Sherbet Syrup. - - 2 "
Mix.

---

## NO. 57.

### MOUNTAIN DEW.

Brandy - - ½ pt.
Ess. Nutmeg - - 1 oz.
Extract Vanilla - 1 "
*Phospho-Guarana Syrup* 1 pt.
Fruit Acid - - ½ oz.
Gum Foam - - 1 "
Simple Syrup, enough for 1 gal.
Mix and color to suit.

### NO. 58.
#### MOUNTAIN PINK.

| | |
|---|---|
| Phospho-Guarana Syrup | 1 pt. |
| Spts, Juniper | 4 ozs. |
| Lemon Syrup | 1 pt. |
| Fruit Acid | 1 oz. |
| Gum Foam | 1 " |
| Simple Syrup, enough for | 1 gal. |

Mix.

### NO. 59.
#### MEXICAN SARSAPARILLA.

| | |
|---|---|
| Fruit Acid | ¾ oz. |
| Essence Sarsaparilla | ¼ " |
| Fld. Ext. Gentian (plain | ¼ " |
| Fld. Ext. Sarsaparilla (comp) | ¼ " |
| Gum Foam | 1 " |
| Caramel enough to color. | |
| Simple Syrup | 1 gal. |

Mix. *This syrup is similar to* **Moxie** *and is a good seller. Try it.*

### NO. 60.
#### ESSENCE LEMON.

Take

| | |
|---|---|
| Oil of Lemon, Sanderson's | 1 oz. |
| Lemon Peel, freshly grated, | ⅝ oz. |
| Alcohol enough for | 16 oz. |

Dissolve the oil in 14 oz. of the alcohol, add the lemon peel, and allow to macerate for 24 hours, then filter through filter paper, and add enough alcohol through the filter to make 1 pint. This makes a very fine Lemon Essence, and for bottlers' use is especially fine. 3 oz. to 1 gallon syrup, colored with a little Tr. Curcuma, and the addition of 1 oz. of Fruit Acid and 1-2 oz. Gum Foam makes a fine Lemon Syrup.

---

### NO. 61.

#### ESSENCE PEPPERMINT.

Oil Peppermint - - 1½ ozs.
Peppermint in coarse pow-
    der - - 60 grains.
Alcohol enough for 16 oz.

Macerate and proceed as in making Lemon Essence.

---

### NO. 62.

#### ESSENCE FOR MEXICAN SARSAPARILLA.

Oil Wintergreen - - 1 oz.
Oil Sassafras - - 1 "
Alcohol 4 "
    Mix.

## NO. 63.

### NECTAR EXTRACT NO. 1.

Oil Rose (Kiss) - 6 drops.
Oil Bitter Almonds - 6 "
Vanilla Extract    1½ ozs.
Lemon Oil - - 60 drops.
Alcohol - - 1 oz.
   Mix.

## NO. 64.

### NECTAR SYRUP NO. 1.

Extract Nectar, . . ¼ oz.
Raspberry Juice . . 6 "
Gum Foam . . 1 "
Fruit Acid, . , . ½ "
Simple Syrup, enough for 1 gal.

## NO. 65.

### NECTAR SYRUP NO. 2.

Strawberry Syrup, . . 1 qt.
Orgeat Syrup, . , 1 "
Madeira Wine, . . 4 oz.
Gum Foam . . ½ "
   Mix.

## NO. 66.

### NECTARINE.

| | |
|---|---|
| Nectar Syrup, | ½ gal. |
| Lemon Syrup, | 1 pt. |
| Vanilla Syrup, | 1 " |
| Simple Syrup enough for | 1 gal. |
| Gum Foam | ¼ oz. |

Color with Fruit Color.
Mix.

## NO. 67.

### ORGEAT SYRUP.

| | |
|---|---|
| Ess. Almonds | 44 drops. |
| Simple Syrup | 3 qts. |
| Gum Foam | ¾ oz. |

Mix.

## NO. 68.

### ORANGE SYRUP.

| | |
|---|---|
| Extract Orange, Saxe's formula or B. & C's. | 1½ oz. |
| Fruit Acid | ½ " |
| Gum Foam | 1 " |
| Simple Syrup | 1 gal. |

Mix. This is fine.

### NO. 69.

**SAXE'S ORANGE EXTRACT (UNEQUALED).**

Grated Peel of 60 Oranges.
Water - - - 3 qts.
Alcohol - - 3 "
Glycerine - - - 6 ozs.

Macerate from two to four weeks, then add oil orange best, 1 ounce, and then strain through flannel. This makes the finest orange flavor for orange syrup and for orange phosphate I have ever used, and at about one-third the cost of any other first-class extract in the market.

### NO. 70.

**ORANGE SHERBET.**

Orange Syrup - - 1 qt.
Sherbet Syrup - - - 1 "
Mix and draw still.

### NO. 71.

**BLOOD ORANGE PHOSPHATE SYRUP.**

*Best in the Market.*

Raspberry Juice, A. H. P.'s 6 oz.
Extract of Orange,
        B. & C's. - 1½ "
Fruit Acid - - - ¾ "

Simple Syrup enough for   1 gal.
    Mix.  Cactucine color few drops.

The combination of the raspberry juice with the orange extract makes the finest flavored orange phosphate in the world. The acid phosphate is added when the drink is served. My customers often ask why my orange phosphate is so much finer than that made by other dispensers. The reason is, we know how to make it.

### NO. 72.

#### OPERA BOUQUET.

| | |
|---|---|
| Phospho-Guarana | 1 pt. |
| Simple Syrup | 1 pt. |
| Sherry Wine | 1 pt. |
| One Lemon cut in thin slices | |

    Mix and allow to stand 12 hours, then strain and add

| | |
|---|---|
| Gum Foam | ⅓ oz. |
| Fruit Acid | ¼ " |

### NO. 73.

#### PINEAPPLE SYRUP NO. 1.

| | |
|---|---|
| Pineapple Juice (the best) | 12 oz. |
| Fruit Acid | ½ " |

Gum Foam - - - 1 "
Simple Syrup enough for 1 gal.
This gives the true flavor of the pineapple.

### NO. 74.

#### PINEAPPLE SYRUP NO. 2.

*Cheaper than No. 1, and Very Good.*
Fruit Juice of Pineapple 6 oz.
Fruit Acid - - - ½ "
Extract of Pineapple - ½ "
Gum Foam - - - 1 "
Syrup enough for - 1 gal.
 Mix.

### NO. 75.

#### RASPBERRY SYRUP NO. 1.

Raspberry Juice - 12 oz.
Fruit Acid - - - 3-8 "
Gum Foam - - 1 "
Simple Syrup enough for 1 gal.
Fruit Color, a few drops.
 Mix.

## NO. 76.

### RASPBERRY SYRUP NO. 2.

Raspberry Juice . - 6 oz.
Extract Raspberry - ½ "
Fruit Acid - - 3-8"
Gum Foam - - - 1 "
Simple Syrup - - 1 gal.
Mix.

## NO. 77.

### RAZZLE DAZZLE SYRUP.

Nectar Syrup . . 1 pt.
Strawberry Syrup . . 1 "
Lemon Syrup . . ½ "
Phospho-Guarana Syrup . ½ "
Jamaica Ginger Wine . ½ "
Essence Nutmeg . . 15 drops.
Simple Syrup enough for 1 gal.
Mix.

## NO. 78.

### ROOT BEER.

Boston Root Ext. (B. & C.'s) 6 oz.
Gum Foam . . . ½ "
Fruit Acid . . . ½ "
Syrup . . - 1 gal.

Caramel, a few drops.

To charge in fountain, use 1½ gals. above syrup to 7½ gals. water, and charge.

---

### NO. 79.

#### STRAWBERRY SYRUP NO. 1.

Pure Fruit Juice of Strawberries . . . 12 oz.
Fruit Acid . . . ½ "
Gum Foam . . 1 "
Simple Syrup enough for 1 gal.
Mix. Cactucine, B. & C's. few drops.

---

### NO. 80.

#### STRAWBERRY SYRUP NO. 2.

Strawberry Juice . 6 oz.
Ext. Strawberry . . ½ "
Fruit Acid . . . ½ "
Gum Foam . . . 1 "
Syrup Simplex . . 1 gal.
Fruit Color, a few drops.
   Mix.

## NO. 81.

### SWIZZLE FIZZ SYRUP.

| | |
|---|---|
| Jamaica Ginger Wine (Puffer's) | 1 qt. |
| Phospho-Guarana Syrup | 1 " |

Mix, and draw mineral glass ⅞ full plain soda, add one ounce above syrup, a little acid phosphate and small teaspoonful powdered sugar. *Stir.* Good drink in the morning.

---

## NO. 82.

### SOLFERINO.

| | |
|---|---|
| Wild Grape Juice | 6 oz. |
| Strawberry Syrup | 1 pt. |
| Phospho-Guarana Syrup | 1 " |
| Gum Foam | 1 oz. |
| Fruit Acid | ¼ " |
| Simple Syrup enough for | 1 gal. |

Mix.

---

## NO. 83.

### SHERBET NO. 1.

| | |
|---|---|
| Port Wine | 8 oz. |
| Catawba Wine | 8 " |
| Vanilla Syrup | 2 pt. |
| Pineapple Syrup | 2 " |

Gum Foam , . , 1 oz.
Fruit Acid . . ¼ "
Mix. This makes a very pleasant drink.

### NO. 84.

#### SHERBET NO. 2.

Vanilla Syrup . . . 3 pt.
Pineapple Syrup . . . 1 "
Lemon Syrup . , . 1 "
Gum Foam . - ½ oz.
Fruit Acid . , . ½ "
Mix.

### NO. 85.

#### SARSAPARILLA SYRUP.

Ext. Sarsaparilla . . ¼ oz.
Gum Foam . . 1 "
Fruit Acid . . ¼ "
Caramel to color.
Simple Syrup , . 1 gal.
Mix.

### NO. 86.

#### EXTRACT SARSAPARILLA.

*For Sarsaparilla Syrup.*

Oil Wintergreen . . 1 oz.
Oil Sassafras . . . 1 "

Alcohol . . . 6 oz.
Caramel, a few drops.
Mix.

---

### NO. 87.

### VANILLA SYRUP.

Extract Vanilla . . 1½ oz.
Fruit Acid . . ¼ "
Gum Foam . . . 1 "
Simple Syrup enough for 1 gal.
Mix.

---

### NO. 88.

### VANILLA CREAM SYRUP.

Extract Vanilla, . . . 1 oz.
Simple Syrup, . . . . 3 pt.
Rich Milk, . . . . 1 "
Mix.

---

### NO. 89.

### WILD GRAPE.

Wild Grape Juice (A. H. Peloubet's) 10 oz.
Fruit Acid, . . . ½ "
Gum Foam, . . . . 1 "
Simple Syrup enough for . . 1 gal.
Mix.

### NO. 90.

#### FANCY MIXED DRINKS.

In making fancy drinks, such as Egg Phosphate, Egg Lemonade, Plain Lemonade, etc., it is necessary to have a small outfit for mixing, consisting of a long nickel or silver plated shaker, one long silver mixing spoon, one 12-ounce mixing glass, one spoon strainer and one lemon squeezer. In some of these drinks we use carbonated water, and in others simply filtered water. As carbonated water cannot be shaken in the "mixer," we use cracked ice with the drinks that require carbonated water, and pour back and fourth from the mixing glass into the mixer, till the drink is in good shape, then strain and serve.

### NO. 91.

#### ALMOND SPONGE.

Put about 1 ounce Orgeat Syrup in mixing glass, fill half full cracked ice, add about a teaspoonful powdered sugar and enough Strawberry syrup to color, then fill the glass with fresh milk, and shake the mixture thoroughly till you have a rich creamy foam on the top about an inch deep, then strain into soda glass, holding the shaker containing the liquid as high as possible over the glass to put a *bead* on the drink. After drink is made, shake a little powdered nutmeg on top, and it is ready to serve.

The above rule for mixing will apply to nearly all fancy drinks, except when using carbonated waters, then in place of shaking the mixture, pour from one glass to the other.

### NO. 92.

#### BOSTON FLIP.

Use one ounce Don't Care Syrup, one whole egg, teaspoonful lemon juice, half teaspoonful acid phosphate, teaspoonful sugar (or more if necessary), a little cracked ice. Then fill glass with plain soda and proceed as in making almond sponge, only do not shake the drink.

### NO. 93.

#### CHOCOLATE PHOSPHATE.

One ounce Chocolate Syrup, little Acid Phosphate, cracked ice and plain soda; no nutmeg.

### NO. 94.

#### COCA PHOSPHATE..

Syrup Coca 1 ounce, Acid Phosphate, cracked ice, plain soda; no nutmeg.

## NO. 95.

### COCA PHOSPHATE SYRUP.

Coca Phosphate (made by Coca
    Phosphate Co., Chicago)    4 oz.
Simple Syrup   .   .   . 2 qt.
Gum Foam   .   .   . ½ oz.
   Mix.

---

## NO. 96.

### COCA EGG PHOSPHATE.

One ounce Syrup Coca Phosphate, 1 egg, a little Acid Phosphate, cracked ice and plain soda. Mix same as Boston flip.

---

## NO. 97.

### CHARLOTTE RUSSE.

One ounce Don't Care Syrup, ¼ ounce Orgeat Syrup; cracked ice, two small pieces. Fill the glass with milk, and shake thoroughly; then strain, and on top of this put about a tablespoonful of whipped cream, then a little nutmeg, and serve, putting a spoon in glass for customer.

### NO. 98.

#### COFFEE BOUSSHEA.

Coffee Extract (concentrated) 1½ ounce, little cracked ice, tablespoonful sugar ; then fill the glass with milk, shake well, strain, and serve with a little nutmeg.

---

### NO. 99.

#### COFFEE EXTRACT (CONCENTRATED).

Mocha and Java (equal parts, ground), 1 pound. Moisten with 8 ounces of hot water, pack in a cylindrical percolator, and pour on sufficient boiling water to make the finished extract measure one quart ; then bottle and keep in a cool place.

---

### NO. 100.

#### SAXE'S CREAM SHAKE.

*Very Fine.*

Take 1¼ ounces Don't Care Syrup, a little cracked ice. Fill the glass with half milk and half cream, shake very hard for two or three minutes, strain into a long, thin mineral glass, if convenient, and then add a little grated nutmeg. This makes a very rich and especially pleasant drink for the ladies. Cream and milk shakes are made in many ways by the different dispensers, some using one flavor and some another, while the majority give the customers any flavor they ask for, or rather ask them what flavor they would like. This is a mistake. First: Because the customer hardly ever knows what flavor to ask for, or what makes a good combination; second, because it wastes lots of valuable time waiting for the customer to decide; and third, if you have your own combination and stick to it, you will have a little different drink from your competitor, and if the combination is a good one, will work up a nice trade on Milk and Cream Shakes. I use my Don't Care Syrup in both of these drinks, because it makes a combination that is hard to beat, and my customers seem to appreciate it.

I sell my "Milk Shake" for 10 cents, while my competitors sell for 5 cents, yet I sell more Milk Shakes in one day than all the others put together. Cream shake I get 15 cents for.

### NO. 101.

#### EGG DRINKS.

*And How to Make Them Correctly.*

Why is it, in calling for an Egg Phosphate or Egg Lemonade, that at about half the soda fountains they will serve you what we call a sloppy drink—dead and tasteless? One reason is, the dispenser uses too much ice in shaking up the egg with the syrup; the other is, he takes too much time in pouring from glass to shaker and from shaker to glass. Often you will see two men at the same fountain mixing drinks, and using the same material, and while one will make a first-class Egg Drink, that will be relished by the customer, the other will produce such a poor, sloppy mixture that it can hardly be drank. The reason of this is simple enough. The first dispenser has learned the art of mixing properly, while the second has not, and, while they both use the same material in mixing, and from the same apparatus, the results obtained are widely different.

### NO. 102.

#### HOW AN EGG DRINK SHOULD BE MIXED.

First take your mixing-glass in the left hand, and, with the right, put into the glass a lump of ice about the size of a chestnut. Set the glass on the counter; take an egg in right hand between the forefinger and thumb, give it one tap lightly on edge of glass, just enough to crack the shell nicely, but not hard enough to break the yolk of the egg (learn by practice to be able to crack the egg enough the first tap

First three positions in mixing Egg Drinks.

you make); then open the shell quickly, using both hands (see cut), and allow the inside to drop in the glass. At once drop the shell into a bucket under the counter, and don't allow the white to drip on to the counter. Next add about 1½ oz. of Lemon Syrup, or whatever syrup you wish (depends, of course, on which Egg Drink you are making); then put on shaker and shake thoroughly, in the manner shown in cut on another page of this book. When thoroughly shaken, take out the glass (empty) and leave on the counter, egg and syrup being in the shaker; hold the shaker, with contents, under draught arm (soda), and, using the fine stream, fill the shaker about two-thirds full; then use the coarse stream till the shaker is full. Now pour from shaker to glass, repeating the operation three times only. When pouring the last time from shaker to glass, just before serving, while shaker is nearly full, pour fast, holding shaker near the glass, but when the glass is nearly full hold the shaker higher and pour slowly, making a fine stream, which will top off the glass nicely. Next shake a very little nutmeg on top, and the drink is ready to serve.

Many dispensers think they must use lots of ice, which in itself deadens the drink, all being necessary is enough to break the yolk of the egg. Then they often pour the drink too many times from glass to shaker and back again, and, to show off, hold the shaker too high above their head, and too far from the glass, which results in forcing all the gas out, and making the drink flat and tasteless. A first-class soda man throws the drink from shaker to glass, but does not pour it like pouring water from a tumbler into a basin.

It is unnecessary, after shaking the egg, ice and syrup together, to use a strainer, as the ice is nearly all melted by that time, and if you are rushed and time is any object, you will find by dispensing with the strainer, and making your Egg Drink according to my rule, you will save much valuable time.

An Egg Drink should be light and creamy, not heavy and sloppy, and the only way to make the drink properly is to remember : first, don't use too much ice; 2d, don't pour too long ; 3rd, do not use a strainer.

Egg Drinks are quite popular, and very profitable, when properly made and served, but from the fact that there are so many would-be soda men in the business, who know scarcely anything about mixing, and think they know it all, the trade is a little skeptical about trying Egg Drinks, unless they are acquainted with the dispenser.

Second three positions in mixing Egg Drinks.

I have always made a great specialty of Egg Drinks, because they are profitable to me, and I consider very healthful to the customer. Customers often ask me why it is my Egg Drinks taste so much nicer than at other places. The reason is, I always insist on my new dispensers (whether experts or not) learning my way of mixing and serving, and then I feel pretty sure of giving satisfaction.

One very essential feature of success in running a soda fountain is to be able to mix a drink daintily, correctly and quickly, and the soda men who can do this are worth a good salary every time, but they are very scarce, and hard to get.

### NO. 103.

#### EGG PHOSPHATE.

Lemon Syrup 1 ounce, Acid Phosphate 1 teaspoonful, 1 egg, 1 lump of ice; shake well together before adding the soda, to thoroughly mix the egg with the syrup; then add the plain soda and pour from glass to shaker three or four times; add little nutmeg. This rule will apply in making all Egg Drinks.

### NO. 104.

#### EGG LEMONADE.

Take the juice of 1 Lemon, 1 whole egg, about 1 ounce Lemon Syrup, a little cracked ice; shake well, then add soda, using a little nutmeg on top.

### NO. 105.

#### EGG-NOG.

One ounce Don't Care Syrup, ½ ounce Jamaica Ginger Wine, cracked ice, a little sugar, 1 egg; shake well, then add enough milk to fill the glass, and shake again; strain, grate a little nutmeg on top, and serve.

### NO. 106.

#### EGG CHOCOLATE.

Chocolate Syrup 1 ounce, 1 egg, cracked ice; shake, and add plain soda, and proceed as in making Egg Phosphate.

Last three positions in mixing Egg Drinks.

### NO. 107.

#### EGG CALISAYA.

Lemon Syrup 1 ounce, Elixir Calisaya Bark 1 teaspoonful, Phospho-Guarana Syrup ½ oz., a little Acid Phosphate, 1 egg, cracked ice; shake well, then add plain soda, strain and serve with nutmeg.

### NO. 108.

#### EGG FLIP.

One egg, cracked ice, ½ ounce Lemon Syrup, 1 ounce Phospho-Guarana Syrup, 1 teaspoonful Acid Phosphate; shake and add soda, same as in Egg Phosphate.

### NO. 109.

#### FROZEN CREAM.

This drink is made the same as a Cream Shake. Only leave the ice in the glass, using very fine cracked ice, and serve with a spoon. Serve in a long, thin mineral glass, and if in season use one or two strawberries on top, and a little whipped cream.

### NO. 110.

**FLOWING STREAM.**

Mountain Dew Syrup 1 ounce, Orgeat Syrup 1½ ounce, cracked ice, pure milk; shake and strain, use nutmeg.

---

### NO. 111.

**ROYAL CABINET.**

*A Chicago Drink.*

Orange Syrup 1 ounce, Catawba Syrup ½ ounce, 1 egg, ½ ounce cream, lump ice, Carbonated Water; mix and serve same as other egg Drinks.

This drink had quite a run in Chicago during last season—1892—though I think the name had a great deal to do with the sale of it.

---

### NO. 112.

**TACOMA.**

Tonic Syrup 1½ ounces (made from 1 pint Port Wine and 1 gallon Syrup), one egg, little lemon juice, cracked ice, plain soda, little nutmeg. Another Chicago drink.

## NO. 113.

### RAZZLE-DAZZLE.

My own compound, and very popular with both sexes in Chicago last season during the exceeding hot weather. A thirst-quencher.

Take ½ ounce Pine Apple Syrup, teaspoonful lemon juice, teaspoonful raspberry vinegar, then fill the glass two-thirds full of fine cracked ice, put a mixing-spoon in glass, and turn on the coarse stream of soda. Stir with spoon after having filled the glass within about one-fourth of the top with plain soda; add more fine ice, heaping it on top of the glass; then on top of all put about a teaspoonful of crushed raspberry, and stick a small slice of orange between ice and glass. Serve with straws. Serve in ordinary thin soda glasses.

---

## NO. 114.

### GOLDEN FIZZ.

Don't Care Syrup 1 ounce, Phospho-Guarana Syrup ½ ounce, Jamaica Ginger Wine ½ ounce, one whole egg, teaspoonful Acid Phosphate, cracked ice, shake, add soda and strain; use nutmeg.

## NO. 115.

### ICE CREAM SHAKE.

Mix same as Cream Shake, and add heaping teasponful of ice cream.

## NO. 116.

### LIME JUICE FLIP.

Lime Juice ½ ounce, Syrup of Phospho-Guarana 1 ounce, 1 whole egg, cracked ice, teaspoonful Acid Phosphate, tablespoonful sugar, shake and then add soda; strain and then add nutmeg. Then serve.

## NO. 117.

### MILK SHAKE.

Don't Care Syrup 1 ounce, cracked ice half glass, milk enough to fill glass, shake thoroughly; then strain and add a little grated nutmeg. This makes the finest Milk Shake in the country.

## NO. 118.

### MINT JULIP.

Fill glass half full of cracked ice, add teaspoonful powdered sugar, a few sprigs of fresh mint, press to side of glass to get the flavor, add 1 ounce of Don't Care Syrup, then fill the glass with soda and stir with spoon. Don't shake. Add one or two fresh strawberries or a piece of orange; leave ice in glass and let customer use your strainer when drinking.

### NO. 119.

#### ORGEAT A LA EGG.

Orgeat Syrup 1 ounce, little cracked ice, 1 whole egg; proceed same as in making Egg Phosphate.

### NO. 120.

#### PUNCHINE.

One ounce Syrup of Punchine, little cracked ice, milk. Shake, strain and add nutmeg.

### NO. 121.

#### PUNCHINE SYRUP.

Punchine Extract (B. & C.'s) 8 ounces, Fruit Acid ½ ounce, Simple Syrup enough for 1 gallon. Color with Fruit Color. Mix.

### NO. 122.

### *Mint Freeze.*

Take ½ oz. Ginger Fruit Syrup, ½ oz. Raspberry Syrup, ¼ oz. Raspberry Vinegar, ½ oz. Don't Care Syrup, a few sprigs of fresh Mint. Put the syrups in the glass first, then add the Mint, and with a spoon press same to side of glass to get the flavor. Then fill the glass nearly full of cracked ice; next add plain soda, stirring with spoon, and top off with more cracked ice and a little fruit; also a sprig of Mint. Serve in long, thin mineral glasses, with straws.

We get 15 cents for this drink, not on account of the cost (which is small), but on account of the time required in mixing and serving it.

It is a fine drink for a leader, and will draw trade when first introduced.

---

### NO. 123.

### CREAM PUFF.

Coxe's Gelatine 2½ boxes, the whites of ten eggs, ½ gallon simple Syrup, 1 ounce Extract Orange, ½ teaspoonful Cactucine, B. & C.'s, to color, 9½ gallons water. Dissolve the gelatine in hot water. Beat the eggs up thoroughly, mix with the gelatine, then add Syrup and Extract and put in fountain. Then add the water and shake thoroughly. Charge to a pressure of 100 pounds.

### NO. 124.

#### HOW TO DISPENSE CREAM PUFF.

Draw 1½ ounces Orange Syrup and fill the glass about one-half full with plain soda; then take another glass and fill about one-half full of Cream Puff; pour the two together from glass to glass until thoroughly mixed.

This makes a showy drink, and in some localities has a big run. It is a cheap drink and will pay to push.

### NO. 125.

#### SAXE'S PINEAPPLE GLACÉ.

*Very Popular in the South.*

12 ounces Pineapple Juice,
½ gallon Syrup,
2 ozs. Coxe's Gelatine (dissolved in a little hot water),
1 pint Grated Pineapple,

1 oz. Fruit Acid,
5 quarts pure water.

Put into a four-gallon ice cream freezer and freeze same as ice cream. Serve in long-stem cocktail glasses, with after-dinner coffee spoon, and put a strawberry in center on top.

This, of course, is not a drink, but is nevertheless a fine leader, and will draw trade wherever introduced. It costs little to make, and affords a handsome profit for the labor required in making it.

### NO. 126.

#### GOLDEN ADE.

Take the yolk of one egg, 1½ ounces Catawba Syrup, a little cracked ice; shake. Fill the glass with milk, and shake again. Strain, and serve in long, thin mineral glass.

### NO. 127.

#### SILVER ADE.

This drink is made the same as a Golden Ade, only use the white instead of the yolk of the egg.

### NO. 128.

#### CLARET PUNCH.

1 quart St. Julien Claret,
1 pint Catawba Syrup,
½ pint Catawba Wine,
Juice of six lemons,
Sliced lemons, four;
Sliced oranges, four;
8 ounces Raspberry Syrup,
4 ounces Raspberry Cordial,
2 gallons water.

Add sugar to suit the taste. Serve in large punch bowl.

---

### NO. 129.

#### FLOATING ISLAND PUNCH.

2 quarts Catawba Syrup,
1 pint Sherry Wine,
1 pint Simple Syrup,
½ pint fresh strawberries,
½ pint crushed peaches.

On top of this put about a quart of nice rich whipped cream, and drop on top of the cream a few strawberries. Serve as a syrup from the punch bowl, using about 1½ ounces, and draw soda on top, using sweet cream or ice cream, as desired.

Floating Island Punch, when properly made, is very attractive, and will sell itself without advertising, if allowed to stand in punch bowl on top of dispensing counter.

### NO. 130.
### PINEAPPLE SMASH.

Pineapple Syrup 1 ounce, powdered sugar 1 teaspoonful; cracked ice, Lemon Juice 1 teaspoonful; add enough plain soda to fill glass nearly full. Stir with spoon, then add more fine shaved ice till glass is heaping full; then add a little grated pineapple, thin slice of lemon, sprig of fresh mint, one strawberry and two straws. Serve.

### NO. 131.
### RASPBERRY CORDIAL.

Raspberry Vinegar 1 ounce, Raspberry Syrup 1 ounce, little cracked ice; fill glass with soda, stir with spoon and strain into mineral glass.

### NO. 132.
### RASPBERRY VINEGAR.

| | |
|---|---|
| Raspberry Juice | 8 ozs. |
| Cider Vinegar | 2 " |

Mix.

### NO. 133.

#### ROMAN PUNCH.

Tumbler half full cracked ice, Don't Care Syrup one ounce, teaspoonful Lemon Juice, juice of half an orange, teaspoonful sugar; add soda, mix with spoon, and then top off with shaved ice. Add strawberry or a piece of pineapple, and a sprig of mint.

---

### NO. 134.

#### SILVER FIZZ.

Don't Care Syrup 1 ounce, Phospho-Guarana one ounce, the white of an egg, little cracked ice, teaspoonful Lemon Juice. Shake well and add half milk and half soda to fill glass.

Mix same as Egg Phosphate and strain, adding a little nutmeg.

---

### NO. 135.

#### SHERBET DE EGG.

Sherbet Syrup 1 ounce, 1 whole egg, a little Lemon Juice, little Acid Phosphate, cracked ice. Shake. Add soda and strain.

### NO. 136.

#### STRAWBERRY GLACÉ.

Make same as Pineapple Smash, only use Strawberry Syrup instead of Pineapple.

---

### NO. 137.

#### SELTZER LEMONADE.

Juice of one whole lemon, tablespoonful sugar, little cracked ice; stir with spoon, add Seltzer Water, stir again and strain.

---

### NO. 138.

#### TULIP PEACH.

Make the same as Strawberry Glacé, using Peach Syrup in place of Strawberry.

---

### NO. 139.

#### VICHY EGG SHAKE.

Take 1 whole egg, little cracked ice, and about 1 ounce of filtered water, Shake thoroughly and strain into tall mineral glass; then add Vichy Water slowly until glass is full, stirring with spoon while drawing the Vichy. This is a great morning drink.

### NO. 140.

#### STILL DRINKS.

These are made by drawing Soda first and then adding the Syrup, stirring with a spoon and serving in mineral glass.

For instance, in making

---

### NO. 141.

#### ORANGEADE.

Draw mineral glass ⅞ full plain Soda; then add Orange Syrup 1 ounce, Lemon Juice 1 teaspoonful and stir with spoon; then serve.

Pineapple, Strawberry, Raspberry, Cranberry, etc., are made in the same way.

---

### NO. 141½.

#### WILD CHERRY PHOSPHATE.

*Very Fine and a Popular Drink.*

Wild Cherry Extract (B. & C,'s) 4 ozs.
Simple Syrup . . . 1 gal.
Fruit Acid . . . . 1 oz.
Caramel enough to color slightly.

Mix, and serve as a still drink in an eight-ounce mineral glass, adding the Phosphate last, **and** stirring with a spoon.

## NO. 142.

### SOUR DRINKS.

These are served still, like the "Ades," in mineral glass, but contain beside the Syrup either Phosphate, Lemon Juice, Lime Juice or Lactart.

---

## NO. 143.

### CRANBERRY PHOSPHATE.

*Very Fine.*

| | |
|---|---|
| Plain Soda | 7 oz. |
| Cranberry Syrup | 1 " |
| Acid Phosphate | 1 teasp'n |

Mix and serve.

---

## NO. 144.

### CRANBERRY SYRUP.

| | |
|---|---|
| Cranberry Juice | 10 oz. |
| Fruit Acid | 1 " |
| Gum Foam | 1 " |
| Simple Syrup, | 1 gal. |

Mix.

First two positions in making Still Drinks.

### NO. 145.

### LEMON PHOSPHATE.

Serve same as above, using Lemon instead of Cranberry Syrup.

---

### NO. 146.

### LACTART.

This is an Acid similar to the Acid Phosphate, made in Boston, and put up in ½ pint bottles. It can be used in same proportion as Acid Phosphate in making Still Drinks. Lemon and Orange Lactart are very nice drinks.

---

### NO. 147.

### "SAXE'S ORANGE PHOSPHATE."

*The Great and only true Orange Phosphate made.*

Plain Soda. . . 7 oz.
Saxe's Blood Orange Syrup, 1 "
Acid Phosphate, . 1 teaspoon.
Mix.

### NO. 148.

#### PINEAPPLE PHOSPHATE.

Plain Soda . . 7 oz.
Pineapple Syrup . 1 "
Acid Phosphate or Lactart, 1 teaspoon.
   Mix.

Peach, Strawberry, Raspberry, etc., are made in the same way.

---

### NO. 149.

#### VICHY PHOSPHATE.

Draw mineral glass nearly full Vichy water; then add teaspoonful Acid Phosphate. Stir with spoon and serve.

---

### NO. 150.

#### LEMON ICE.

Juice of 10 Lemons.
Fruit Acid . . . 1 oz.
Granulated Sugar . . 3 lbs.
Cox's Gelatine (dissolved in hot
  water) . . . 1 Box.
Water enough to make . 1 gal.
   Mix, and freeze in 2 gal. Ice Cream Freezer. Serve in small thin glass mug, or in a cocktail glass.

Last two positions in making Still Drinks.

### NO. 151.

#### ORANGE ICE.

Juice of 3 Lemons.
Juice of 10 Oranges.
Extract Orange . . 1 oz.
Fruit Acid . . 1 "
Cox's Gelatine . . 1 box.
Water enough for . . 1 gal.
Granulated Sugar . . 3 lbs.

   Mix. Freeze and serve same as Lemon Ice.

---

### NO. 152.

#### TONIC DRINKS—NO. 1.

*Angostura.*

Plain Soda . . . 7 ozs.
Simple Syrup . . . 1 oz.
Angostura Bitters, about . 20 drops.
Acid Phosphate . . . few drops.
   Mix and serve.

#### No. 2.

*Calisaya.*

Plain Soda . . . 7 ozs.
Lemon Syrup . . . 1 oz.
Elixir Calisaya Bark . ⅛ "
Acid Phosphate . few drops.
   Mix and serve.

No. 3.

*Coca-Calisaya.*

| Plain Soda | 7 ozs. |
| Syrup Coca Phosphate | 1 oz. |
| Acid Phosphate | few drops. |
| Elixir Calisaya | " " |

Mix and serve.

---

### NO. 153.

#### PERUVIAN OR OTTAWA BEER.

| Peruvian Beer Extract | 8 ozs. |
| Granulated Sugar | 8 lbs. |
| Cold Water | 10 gals. |

Put in a 14-gallon fountain and charge to pressure of 150 pounds. Draw through Mineral Draught Tube into a large pitcher; allow time to settle, then pour out about two-thirds glass full of solid liquid, and fill glass from the Draught Tube.

This makes a very nice drink.

---

### NO. 154.

#### CARBONATED MINERAL WATERS.

There are any number of formulas in the market for making artificial Mineral Waters, but very few of them are worthy of attention.

I give below two formulas which I know from experience *to be* good. It is not necessary to keep on draught more than two carbonated minerals, to be able to serve any kind a customer calls for. Vichy will answer for High Rock, Deep Rock or Seltzer, and Apollinaris for Kissengen or White Rock Water.

### NO. 155.

#### APOLLINARIS WATER.

| | |
|---|---|
| Chloride Soda | 280 gr'ns. |
| Sulphate Soda | 180 " |
| Carbonate Magnesia | 260 " |
| Bi-Carbonate Soda | 760 " |
| Carbonated Water | 4 pts |

Mix, and add to 9½ gallons water; then charge.

### NO. 156.

#### VICHY WATER.

| | |
|---|---|
| Potass Sulphate | 120 gr'ns |
| Sodium ' | 80 " |
| " Phosphate | 50 " |
| " Chloride | 360 " |
| " Bi-carbonate | 2187 " |
| Ammonia Carbonate | 10 " |

Carbonic Acid Water        4 pts

Mix, and let stand for 12 hours; then filter and add to 9½ gallons water. Charge.

### NO. 157.

#### VANILLA ICE CREAM.

| | |
|---|---|
| Granulated Sugar | 1¼ pounds. |
| Whole Eggs | 9 |
| Fresh Milk | 1 gal. |
| Extract Vanilla | 1½ oz. |

Mix sugar and eggs together, using an Egg Beater; add milk and partly freeze before adding the Extract Vanilla.

This will make very nearly two gallons fine Ice Cream, when frozen, and at a much less cost than it can be bought for.

### NO. 158.

#### EXTRACT VANILLA.

| | |
|---|---|
| Vanilla Bean (long) | ¾ oz. |
| Tonka " | ¼ " |
| Granulated Sugar | 1 " |
| Dilute Alcohol | ½ pt. |
| Simple Syrup | ½ " |

Cut the Vanilla and Tonka Bean into small pieces, put in a mortar with the sugar and bruise; then put into a two-quart bottle and allow to macerate for two weeks, shaking the bottle two or three times each day. After that filter and add the Syrup, and enough caramel to give the desired color.

### NO. 159.
#### STRAWBERRY ICE CREAM.

| | |
|---|---|
| Whole eggs | 9 |
| Pure Cream | 2 qts. |
| Granulated Sugar | ½ lb. |
| Milk | 1 qt. |
| Concentrated Syrup Strawberry | 1½ pts. |
| Fruit Acid | ½ oz. |

Beat egg and sugar together thoroughly; add cream and milk, beating thoroughly again; then add the Concentrated Syrup previously mixed with the Fruit Acid and freeze. This makes two gallons very fine Strawberry Ice Cream, and costs on an average, not including labor, about 50 cents per gallon.

### NO. 160.
#### CONCENTRATED STRAWBERRY SYRUP.

| | |
|---|---|
| Strawberry Juice | 12 ozs. |
| Cut Loaf Sugar | 1½ lbs. |

Heat the juice in a porcelain-lined kettle, add the sugar, stir, boil for a moment only and strain; then put in a strong bottle, cork tightly and keep in cool place until used.

### NO. 161.

#### CONCENTRATED PINEAPPLE SYRUP.

Make same as Strawberry Syrup, only use Pineapple Juice.

### NO. 162.

In opening a bottle of fruit juice in hot weather, for making syrup, either make enough syrup to use the entire contents of the bottle, or else make into a concentrated syrup, as the ordinary juice will soon spoil when once opened and exposed to the air.

### NO. 163.

#### CONCENTRATED STRAWBERRY SYRUP MADE FROM FRESH FRUIT.

In seasons when Strawberries are cheap it will pay to make up several gallons of Concentrated Syrup, as there is no Strawberry Juice for sale in the market that can compare with home-made goods for producing the true flavor of the fruit, when made according to my formula.

Take a quantity of dead ripe Strawberries and express the juice from same through *thin* Canton flannel and at once place in porcelain-lined kettle and bring almost to the boiling point, then add cut loaf Sugar in proportions of 1½ lbs. Sugar to 12 ounces of Juice; allow same to dissolve, then bottle and seal in Champagne-shape bottles.

Use in proportion of 1 quart of Concentrated Syrup to 3 quarts plain Syrup for dispensiug.

## NO. 164.

### CONCENTRATED PINEAPPLE SYRUP MADE FROM FRESH FRUIT.

Take two ordinary sized ripe Pineapples, peel off outside, slice in small pieces, put into a large mortar, with about ½ lb. cut loaf Sugar, rub Sugar and Pineapple with pestle, then transfer to porcelain-lined kettle and, after adding 1 lb. more cut loaf Sugar, bring almost to a boil and, after Sugar is all dissolved, strain through strainer cloths and bottle same as Strawberry.

Cherry, Grape and Raspberry Concentrated Syrup made same as Strawberry.

## SAXE'S NEW DRINKS FOR 1894.

### NO. 165.

#### APRIL BLOSSOM.

| | |
|---|---|
| Pine Apple Syrup, | 1 oz |
| Catawba Wine Dry | ½ " |
| Lime Juice | ½ " |
| Raspberry Syrup | ½ " |
| Cracked Ice | ½ glass |
| Lemon Juice | ½ teasp'n |

Use 12-ounce soda glass, add plain soda till glass is three fourths full, (stirring with spoon while adding plain soda,) then fill glass heaping full with cracked ice, and decorate with fruit. Serve with straws.

### NO. 166.

#### MAY BELLS.

| | |
|---|---|
| Klub Soda. | 1 oz. |
| Jamaica Ginger Wine | ½ " |
| Lime Juice | 1½ teasp'n |

Serve in 7-ounce mineral glass. Still.

### NO. 167.

#### JUNE TONIC.

One whole egg.
Cracked Ice
| | | |
|---|---|---|
| Lime Juice | - - | 1 teasp'n |
| Lemon Juice | - - | 1 " |
| Ginger Fruit | - - | 1½ ozs. |
| Jamaica Rum | - - | 2 dashes |

Shake well together, then add plain soda and proceed as in making Egg Phosphate, top off with very little nutmeg.

### NO. 168.

#### JULY BRACER.

| | | |
|---|---|---|
| Raspberry Vinegar | - | ½ oz |
| Catawba Syrup | - - | 1 " |
| Phospho-Guarana Syrup | | ½ " |

Serve still.

### NO. 169.

#### AUGUST VITALIZER.

| | | |
|---|---|---|
| Don't Care Syrup | - | 1 oz |
| Jamaica Rum | - - | 1 teasp'n |
| Lemon Juice | - - | 1 " |
| Egg - - - | - | 1 |
| Klub Soda | - - | ½ oz. |

Cracked ice. Mix, and serve same style as Egg Phosphate.

---

### NO. 170.

#### SEPTEMBER BLESSING.

| | |
|---|---|
| Crab Apple Syrup | ½ oz. |
| Raspberry Cordial | ½ " |
| Ginger Fruit Syrup | 1 " |
| Jamaica Ginger Wine | ½ " |
| Lime Juice | 1 teasp'n |
| Lemon Juice | 1 " |

Cracked Ice.

Serve in Soda Glass same as Pine Apple Smash.

---

### NO. 171.

#### OCTOBER FAVORITE.

| | |
|---|---|
| Klub Soda Syrup | 1 oz. |
| Ginger Fruit Syrup | ½ " |
| Ginger Wine | ¼ " |
| Lime Juice | ⅛ " |

Serve with Carbonated Waters Still, in 7-ounce mineral glass.

### NO. 172.

#### LOUISVILLE PUNCH.

| | |
|---|---|
| Ice Cream | 4 ozs. |
| Don't Care Syrup | 1½ " |
| Jamaica Ginger Wine | ⅛ " |
| Jamaica Rum | ⅛ " |

Cracked Ice; small amount.
Fill glass with sweet milk, shake thoroughly, and serve with little nutmeg on top. Use long, thin 12-ounce glass.

---

### NO. 173.

#### NEW ORLEANS PUNCH.

One whole egg.

| | |
|---|---|
| Cracked Ice | 2 lumps |
| Don't Care Syrup | 1½ ozs. |
| Jamaica Rum | ¼ " |

Milk enough to fill the Glass. Shake thoroughly, strain and serve in thin Soda Glass with nutmeg on top.

---

### NO. 174.

#### CHERRY ORANGE PHOSPHATE.

| | |
|---|---|
| Saxe's Blood Orange Syrup | 1 oz. |
| Wild Cherry Syrup | ½ " |

Acid Phosphate - - 1 teasp'n
Plain Soda.
Serve still in mineral glass.

### NO. 175.

#### GINGERADE.

Jamaica Ginger Wine - ¼ oz.
Raspberry Vinegar - - ¼ "
Ginger Fruit - - 1 "
Plain Soda - - - 5½ "
Mix, and serve still.

### NO. 176.

#### APPLEADE.

Crab Apple Phosphate Syrup 1 oz.
Raspberry Cordial - - ¼ "
Klub Soda - - ¼ "
Plain Soda - - - 5½ "
Mix and serve still.

### NO. 177.

#### NECTINE.

Pine Apple Syrup - 1 oz.
Raspberry Cordial - - ½ "

Acid Phosphate - - 1 teasp'n
Lemon Juice - - - ½ "
Plain Soda - - 5½ ozs.
   Mix, serve still.

---

### NO. 178.
#### ORANGENA.

Plain Orange Syrup - 1 oz.
Orange Juice - - - ¼ "
Lemon Juice - - ⅛ "
Raspberry Cordial - - ¼ "
Plain Soda - - 5½ "
   Mix, and serve still.

## SAXE'S FORMULAS FOR HOT DRINKS.

#### NO. 179.

This branch of the soda business is still in its infancy, but is gaining a little each year, and in towns where the dispenser is justified in running his apparatus all winter it is generally best to sell Hot Drinks; also, as there are only a few Hot Drinks that are really of any account, I shall give *only* my *formulas* for those that are most popular, and that require especial care in mixing. Nearly all the new extracts for hot drinks that are now on the market give the formula on each bottle for mixing, so it will not be necessary for me to include a list of these drinks.

#### NO. 180.

As Hot Soda, or what is called Hot Soda, does not require *Carbonated Water*, but just plain hot water, and the different flavors, it is not absolutely necessary to have an elaborate outfit for dispensing. Either a neat hot water urn, or a counter apparatus with hot water bath, arranged for direct pressure, will do. The more elaborate the apparatus the more attention it draws, same as in Cold Soda Apparatus.

### NO. 181.

### ARTICLES NECESSARY FOR OPERATING A HOT SODA APPARATUS.

1 Cream Pitcher, Sugar Bowl, Chocolate Pitcher, Keystone Cream Whipper, Hot Soda Mugs to hold about 8 ounces, long Handled, Silver Spoons, Salt, Pepper and Nutmeg Sprinklers, Silver or Glass Dish for Whipped Cream.

---

### NO. 182.

The principal Hot Soda drinks, or the ones most popular are: Hot Coffee, Chocolate, Beef, Beef and Celery, Clam Broth, Oyster Juice, Ginger, Lemon and the Egg Drinks. As Coffee and Chocolate are really the leaders, great care should be observed in the matter of small details. It is first necessary and essential to have fine Whipped Cream, for both drinks. The Coffee extract should be the best that can be obtained, also the Chocolate; an ordinary Coffee or Chocolate Syrup such as is used in cold *soda*, will not answer for these two drinks for the reason that in getting the required strength of each flavor, so much syrup would be required it would make the drink too sweet and sickish. If my formulas are *carefully observed good results* will *follow*, and the finest Hot Chocolate and Coffee in the world will be obtained.

### NO. 183.

#### WHIPPED CREAM.

Take about one-half pint of *pure rich sweet cream*, put it on ice for about one hour or till thoroughly chilled, then whip with a Keystone Whipper, until it is so thick and heavy it will stand alone. It is not necessary or best to use sugar or gelatine in whipping cream, provided you can get pure cream. While whipping the cream, keep on ice all the time.

### NO. 184.

#### SAXE'S CONCENTRATED COFFEE EXTRACT.

Take one pound best Mocha and Java Coffee ground coarse, moisten with a little hot water, then put into a half-gallon conical glass percolator, with a small piece of absorbent cotton in the bottom to clear the liquid as it passes through. After putting coffee into percolator insert a cork in small end, or outlet of same, then pour on about four ounces boiling water and allow to stand twenty minutes, covering top of percolator with a plate or anything else suitable for the purpose. After standing twenty minutes remove the cork from small end, and pour on enough more boiling water so that you can percolate enough for one pint, *no more*. What runs through after that will be too weak. Put the extract in a pint bottle, cork and then put on ice till ready to use. This extract will not keep over a week or ten days, unless kept on ice, but is much better; that is, retains the natural aroma of the coffee much better than when alcohol is used for preserving it.

### NO. 185.

#### TO SERVE HOT COFFEE.

Put one tablespoonful (or more if required) Saxe's Coffee Extract in Soda Mug, then add the required amount of cut loaf sugar and sweet cream, if desired; stir with spoon and gradually add the hot water till mug is nearly full, then top off with heaping teaspoonful of Whipped Cream. (The addition of fine Whipped Cream will improve this drink fifty per cent.)

### NO. 186.

#### HOT CHOCOLATE.

Put one-half ounce Yabara Choclate Syrup, (see my formula for same, on page 40), in mug, add teaspoonful sweet cream, then the Hot Water, stirring constantly with spoon till mug is nearly full, then add Whipped Cream on top, same as in Hot Coffee.

Yabara Chocolate Syrup, being so concentrated, will make a very fine Hot Chocolate drink. Another good formula for Hot Chocolate is to use powdered *Soluble Chocolate*, two teaspoonfuls cut loaf sugar to sweeten, then add hot water and Whipped Cream. There are many good manufactures of powdered Soluble Chocolate in the market and you will have no trouble in getting it of your wholesale house.

### NO. 187.

#### HOT LEMON.

Make a Lemon Syrup from my formula for Syrup Lemon cold, only use double the quantity of Oil Lemon, and also use an extra heavy simple syrup. Use one ounce of this syrup to seven *ounces hot water*.

### NO. 188.

#### HOT GINGER SYRUP.

Use double the quantity of Saxe's Ginger Extract in making this Syrup (see formula for

Ginger Extract), and an extra heavy simple syrup. Serve same as Hot Lemon.

### NO. 189.
#### HOT CLAM BROTH.

Two tablespoonfuls Clam Juice, same of sweet milk, then add hot water till mug is full, stir with spoon and add salt and pepper to suit taste.

### NO. 190.
#### HOT CLAM JUICE AND LEMON.

One tablespoonful Clam Juice, one teaspoonful Lemon Juice, hot water enough to fill mug; add salt and pepper.

### NO. 191.
#### HOT BEEF TEA.

Take one-half teaspoonful Liebig's, Armour's or any other reliable solid Beef Extract; put in mug, add hot water slowly till dissolved, then fill mug with hot water, and season to suit taste.

### NO. 192.
#### HOT BEEF AND CELERY.

Two teaspoonfuls liquid Beef and Celery, add hot water, and season to suit taste. Or use one-half teaspoonful Beef Extract (*solid*), cup hot water; then add celery salt, and season to suit the taste.

### NO. 193.

#### HOT OYSTER JUICE.

One ounce fresh juice or liquid taken from top of quantity of Oysters, tablespoonful sweet cream; then fill mug with hot water, and add a small piece of fresh butter, and season with salt and pepper.

### NO. 194.

#### HOT EGG PHOSPHATE.

Break a fresh egg into shaker, add a small piece of ice to break the yolk of the egg in shaking, then add one ounce strong Lemon Syrup, one teaspoonful acid Phosphate; shake thoroughly, then pour into hot soda mug, and add hot water; top off with nutmeg.

### NO. 195.

#### HOT EGG LEMONADE.

Same as Egg Phosphate, only add two teaspoonfuls *Lemon Juice*.

### NO. 196.

#### HOT EGG PUNCH.

*Serve in Long Thick Soda Glass.*

Take four ounces hot milk, one and one-half ounces Saxe's Don't Care Syrup, (see formula for Don't Care Syrup), one whole egg, shake the egg first with the syrup and a little cracked ice, then add the hot milk, and a teaspoonful or more Jamaica Rum, (as may be required), pour from shaker to glass, and back again, four or five times, last pour leave in glass, and after putting glass in holder, add hot water and stir with spoon; top off with nutmeg. This makes a fine drink when a person is feeble or has been exposed to the cold.

---

### NO. 197.

#### MANITOBA PUNCH.

Take one ounce Jamaica Ginger Wine, one tablespoonful French Brandy, one teaspoonful *Vermouth*, eight ounces hot milk, proceed same as in making *Egg Punch.*

---

### NO. 198.

#### HOT LIME JUICE FLIP.

Two teaspoonfuls Lime Juice, one teaspoonful Jamaica Ginger Wine, one ounce and one-half Ginger Fruit Syrup, (see formula for

Ginger Fruit Syrup), one egg; shake the Egg, Syrup and Lime Juice together, then add the Ginger Wine, put into the soda Glass, and add hot water; top off with nutmeg.

### NO. 199.

#### HOT MALTED MILK.

Two teaspoonfuls Malted Milk, add hot water, stir with spoon, then add salt and pepper instead of sugar. This makes a very nice palatable drink (using salt and pepper in place of sugar) for invalids and convalescents.

### NO. 200.

#### HOT NERVINE.

One-half ounce Ginger Fruit Syrup, one ounce Phospho-Guarana Syrup, teaspoonful Lime Juice, add hot water, stir with spoon and serve.

Almost any of our cold drinks can be served *hot* by using same formulas only substituting hot water for cold carbonated water, and then following the general idea as given in the foregoing formulas for hot drinks. However, I hardly think it is advisable or best to have more than ten or fifteen hot drinks on your list, as this number covers nearly all that are really of any account.

## NO. 201.

### FORMULA FOR CLEANING ICE-CREAM SODA GLASSES.

Take ¼ pound Fuller's Earth and rub up with a little water, making a thin paste. Wet a small sponge with the paste and apply to the glass. **Two or three** rubs will be sufficient; then rinse in clean water, and the glass will shine like burnished steel and retain its luster after drying.

I have tried nearly everything in the market for cleaning glasses that have been used in serving ice-cream soda, but never yet found anything that satisfied me until I used Fuller's Earth. Try it. The cost is almost nothing, but the effect is everything.

If my instructions in regard to making *syrups* and in mixing fancy drinks are closely followed, a new man in the business can soon learn to be an expert. A little good common sense and a natural tendency to be neat and quick about your work, with the aid of "*Saxe's Guide,*" is all you need.

---

On the following pages you will find a few advertisements in regard to **Soda** Water Apparatus and Specialties. All first class houses and reliable in **every way.**

# ATTENTION!

The Cut of <u>Saxe's Practical Sink, Ice Box</u> and <u>Drain</u> on page 29 is worth your special attention.

It was designed and built after long and careful study, to produce the best results in keeping glasses clean, and clean running water all the time, when doing a Soda business of from Two to Three Hundred Dollars a day. No other sink ever made can accomplish what this one has done in saving of labor and time, during a big rush. Now in use at some of the largest Soda Stands in Chicago.

(SEE NEXT PAGE.)

We will build you one of Saxe's Practical Sinks, like cut shown on page 29, for prices as stated below:

5 feet long, 12 inches wide, with one Ice Box, one Sink and Corrugated Drain, including Patent Glass Washer. Price, $38.00.

10 feet long, 18 inches wide, 2 Sinks, 2 Patent Glass Washers and 2 Ice Boxes, with Bottle Rings for 16 Bottles and space for Ice Cream. Price, $70.00.

6 feet long, 16 inches wide, 1 Drain in Center, Ice Box, with 6 Bottle Rings at one end and Sink at the other, with 1 Patent Glass Washer. Price, $45.00.

ADDRESS_____

The Saxe Guide Publishing Co.
409 DEARBORN STREET, CHICAGO.

CHICAGO. WAUKESHA.

# ALMANARIS,

## The Peerless Waukesha Water.

Highest Located Spring in Waukesha, Wis., U. S. A.

Main Office. 275 Kinzie St. - **CHICAGO.**

### ALMANARIS GINGER ALE

SUPERIOR TO ALL OTHERS.

### HOW TO MAKE GOOD SODA WATER.

1. Purchase one of our Patent Apparatus for Fountain Charging. It is unequaled for the purpose for which it was designed.
2. Connect the same to one Drum of our Chemically Pure Liquid Carbonic Acid.
3. Shake 2 lbs. of Liquid Carbonic Acid into your Fountain, previously filled with 10 gallons of "Aqua pura" and "Hey Presto."
4. You are in possession of the best Plain Soda dispensed in your city. Write for Catalogue and further particulars.

**LIQUID CARBONIC ACID MANUFACTURING CO.**

| 437-445 Illinois St., Chicago, Ill. | Benvenue Station, Pittsburgh, Pa. | 3417-3427 Bernard St., St. Louis. Mo. |

# STEEL FOUNTAINS.

## The Only Absolutely Safe Fountain in tne Market.

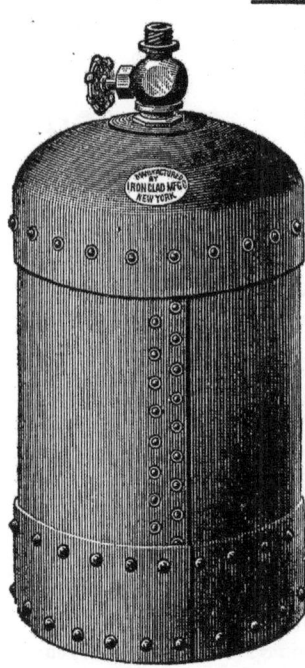

Our STEEL FOUNTAINS have now been on the market for more than twelve years; they have been thoroughly tested, and are pronounced to be the safest and most durable Fountains manufactured. They are made of steel, rolled expressly for the purpose and are lined with extra heavy pure sheet block tin in the most approved manner, insuring absolute protection from contamination.

Owing to the "PECULIAR METHOD" of constructing the ordinary Fountain, the head and bottom cannot be riveted to the cylinder—this explains the statement made by its promoters that "rivets are not necessary." Our NOVEL METHOD of making "Iron Clad" Steel Fountains enables us to use rivets, AND WE USE THEM BECAUSE EXPERIENCE HAS SHOWN THAT FOUNTAINS NOT HAVING THE HEADS AND BOTTOMS RIVETED TO THE CYLINDER ARE LIABLE TO DISASTROUS EXPLOSIONS.

## IRON CLAD MFG. CO.
### 22 Cliff St., N. Y.

**PETER DeLACY, Manager Fountain Department.**

Readers, please mention The Saxe Guide, when writing or buying.

*Fine Drugs  Rare Chemicals  Sponges  Chamois  Tar Camphor Globules  Perfumes  Fruit Juices  Brown's Nickel Glue  Engelhard's Pills  Fenner's Tea*

### HEADQUARTERS FOR

# Vanilla Beans

AND

# Essential Oils

HIGHEST QUALITY
LOWEST PRICES
LARGEST STOCK

WRITE FOR SAMPLES
AND QUOTATIONS

# John Blocki Drug Co.

IMPORTERS AND EXPORTERS.

108 & 110 Randolph St.          CHICAGO.

# SODA WATER APPARATUS
## The Most Modern Dispensing Apparatus.

Excels all others in rapidity, convenience, economy, simplicity and style.
Catalogue mailed, on application, to intending purchasers.

## Chas. Lippincott & Co., Philadelphia, Pa.

BRANCHES: CHICAGO, 341 and 343 Dearborn St.  St. Louis, 1130 Pine St.
San Francisco, 55 Stevenson St.  Boston, 28 Portland St.

# HAVE YOU A SODA APPARATUS?

If so we have a MACHINE that will SAVE you DOLLARS where it COSTS you CENTS.

This is no speculation, it is simply a necessity.

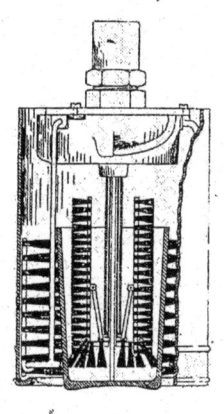

It is a time saver
A money saver
You want it
It is a dandy
Look at it
Order at once
It does the work

Every Soda Fountain should have one. It is the only WASHER and RINSER on the market that will do the work.

Bear in mind that this machine is not merely an ornamental (but useless) rinser, it is a WASHER and a RINSER. Why waste time in washing your glasses in a sink of water that is dirty after five minutes use? Our machine will save you space, labor, time and money. Give your customers clean glasses and instantaneous service, and avoid the accumulation of a sink full of dirty water. It is done by our Machine "in the twinkling of an eye." Does it require warm water? No Sir.

We can wash any soda water glass (cream, chocolate, etc., etc.), in a moment. Does our Machine get out of order? No Sir. Simplicity is one of its cardinal virtues. Brushes furnished for any shape of glass.

**MINIMUM COST.     MINIMUM EFFORT.     MAXIMUM RESULTS.**

You simply insert the glass, press slightly on the bottom and the brushes and water act immediately upon the entire surface of the glass. The moment you withdraw the glass the machine stops, completely shutting off the water.

Endorsed by every one who has used it.

MANUFACTURED BY

## GRAND RAPIDS TUMBLER WASHER CO.

Send for Prices and
Further Particulars.

**GRAND RAPIDS, MICH.**

# TO WHOM IT MAY CONCERN.

This is to certify that I have used the Grand Rapids <u>Tumbler Washer</u> and <u>Rinser</u>, and consider it practical, reliable and a great <u>time saver</u> in cleaning <u>glasses</u> at a Soda Stand. It does the work very thoroughly and without any muss or slop. A good Tumbler Washer at a Soda Stand is as important as good drinks, and clean, neat Dispensers. I take pleasure in recommending this Washer to my friends and patrons.

*Yours for thirst,*
*D. M. Safe*

# GREAT INVENTION

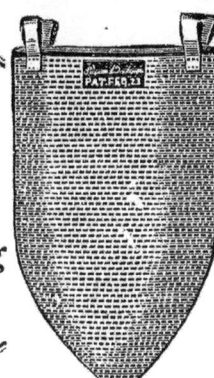

## DERHAMS'
### CELEBRATED PATENT
# FILTER BAGS

Filtering     In Shape

Anything     of Liquids.

## THE VICTOR BAROTHY BOTTLERS SUPPLY CO.
### 409 Dearborn Street, CHICAGO.

**SIZES AND PRICES:**

| | | |
|---|---|---|
| 1 Gallon | | $1.50 |
| 2½ " | | 2.50 |
| 5 " | | 3.75 |
| 8 " | | 5.00 |

### ANY SIZE MADE TO ORDER.

*Felt Filter Bags all Sizes. Send for Price List.*

# Sethness Chemical Co.

### MANUFACTURERS AND DISTILLERS OF
## Pure Fruit Juices and Fountain Extracts

Blackberry, Strawberry, Pineapple, Raspberry, Peach, Orange,
Grape, Lemon, Cherry, Sarsaparilla, Nectar, Banana,
Mead, Vanilla, Acid Phosphate (Comp.) Sparkling Foam,
Fruit Colors, etc,

Our Juices are skillfully prepared from the choicest of Fruit, and equal to any in the market, and are warranted pure and free from any foreign matter. Put up in Champagne Quarts, per doz., $6.00.

In 3 doz. lots, 5 per cent. discount; in 6 doz. lots, 10 per cent. discount. Order through your Wholesale Drug House, or direct

**SETHNESS CHEMICAL CO., 262-8 N. Curtis Street,  -  CHICAGO.**

---

## Rowe's Improved Automatic
## TUMBLER WASHER

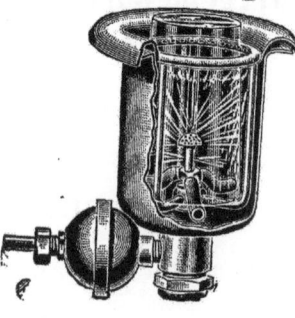

*Washes each Glass with Fresh Water.*
*It will help your trade.*
*Easily Attached. Automatic in Action.*
*Simple as a Faucet.*

**L. L. ROWE**, Manufacturer,

**18 HOWARD ST.,  -  BOSTON, MASS.**

# Rock Candy Syrup

We are the only firm in the United States engaged exclusively in the manufacture of Rock Candy and Rock Candy Syrup.

Every one of our competitors has been compelled to add "side lines to help pay expenses during the dull season," as one of them puts it. We have no "side lines" and no dull season. We are busy all the time manufacturing only two articles—Rock Candy and Triple Refined Rock Candy Syrup.

We allow the retailer a handsome special rebate for quantity; whether he orders our Syrup through his wholesaler or of

## Dryden & Palmer,
## New York.

# SAXE'S
# Phospho-Guarana

## WITH CELERY

Will bring trade that you could never get for ordinary soda.

It's a great Thirst-Quencher and, as the name indicates, is excellent for Nervous or Sick Headache.

People soon learn to like this drink, and will walk out of their way to get it.

Send for a case, and ask for Cloth Banner Sign FREE.

---

Price per Case of One Dozen Quart Bottles, $6

Twenty-five Drinks in each Bottle.

---

**BEACH & CLARRIDGE,**
BOSTON,
Or 324 Dearborn St., CHICAGO.

# Beach & Clarridge,

## BOSTON, MASS.

Wish to inform the public of their Branch at Chicago for the purpose of supplying immediate demands. Will always have in stock a full assortment of the celebrated brand of B. & C. Soda Water Flavors and Fruit Juices. We wish to call especial attention to our Acme Lemon Extract, one ounce to the gallon, which produces a fine Lemon Flavor; also the B. & C. Orange, Ginger Ale Klub Soda, Crab-Apple Juice, Peach Cream and Liq. Chocolates are worthy of your notice.

OFFICE AND SALESROOM
200 to 210 MONON BUILDING
324 Dearborn Street, CHICAGO, ILL.

J. M. HARDER, Agent.

| | NO. |
|---|---|
| Much time and trouble can be saved by using this Index. It gives the number of each formula, *not* the page. **INDEX** Look over this Index carefully, as it will remind you of many profitable and popular drinks that you may want to try. | |

| | NO. |
|---|---|
| Art of mixing | 14 |
| Ades, orange and others | 141 |
| Carbonated water, how made | 6 |
| Cleaning soda glasses | 163 |
| Charging founts | 2–4 |
|     Tuft's formula | 7 |
|     Saxe's " | 8 |
|     Best method | 10 |
| Cream cans | 19 |
| Cream Puff, how to dispense | 124 |
| Drawing soda, how to draw solid | 123 |
| Essence Coffee | 99 |
|     Jamaica ginger | 46 |
|     Lemon | 60 |
|     Nectar No. 1 | 63 |
|     Orange (Saxe's) | 69 |
|     Mexican sarsaparilla | 62 |
|     Peppermint | 61 |
|     Sarsaparilla | 86 |
|     Vanilla | 158 |
| Experience of author | 1 |
| Egg drinks, how to make properly | 101 |
| *Fancy mixed drinks* | 90 |
|     Almond sponge | 91 |

## INDEX.

**Fancy Mixed Drinks.**—*Continued.*     NO.

| | |
|---|---|
| Boston flip | 92 |
| Chocolate phosphate | 93 |
| Claret punch | 128 |
| Coca phosphate | 94 |
| Coca egg phosphate | 96 |
| Charlotte russe | 97 |
| Coffee bousshea | 98 |
| Cream shake | 100 |
| Egg phosphate (Saxe's) | 103 |
|   " lemonade | 104 |
|   " nog | 105 |
|   " chocolate | 106 |
|   " calisaya | 107 |
|   " flip | 108 |
| Frozen cream | 109 |
| Flowing stream | 110 |
| Floating island punch | 129 |
| Golden fizz | 114 |
| Golden ade | 126 |
| Ice-cream shake | 115 |
| Lime juice flip | 116 |
| Milk shake | 117 |
| Mint freeze | 122 |
| Mint julip | 118 |
| Orgeat a la egg | 119 |
| Punchine | 120 |
| Pineapple smash | 130 |
| Pineapple glacé | 125 |
| Raspberry cordial | 131 |

## INDEX.

**Fancy Mixed Drinks.**—*Continued.* NO.

    Raspberry vinegar........................ 132
    Razzle dazzle............................ 113
    Roman punch............................ 133
    Royal cabinet........................... 111
    Silver fizz.............................. 134
    Silver ade.............................. 127
    Sherbet de egg.......................... 135
    Strawberey glacé........................ 136
    Seltzer lemonade........................ 137
    Tacoma................................. 112
    Tulip peach............................ 138
    Vichy egg shake........................ 139

Fountain, how to make attractive............ 25
Fruit acid.................................. 31
Ginger ale (Belfast)........................ 47
Gum foam.................................... 30
How to draw trade........................... 12
How to draw soda............................ 13
How to draw ice-cream soda.................. 14
How not to be out of goods.................. 20
Ices—
    Lemon ice.............................. 150
    Orange ice............................. 151
Ice cream
    Strawberry............................. 150
    Vanilla................................ 157
Ice, shaved, in soda........................ 21
Jamaica ginger wine......................... 52
List of drinks.............................. 27

# INDEX.

| | NO. |
|---|---|
| Mineral water, carbonated | 154 |
| " Apollinaris | 155 |
| " Vichy | 156 |
| Opening bottled fruit juices | 162 |
| Peruvian or Ottawa Beer | 153 |
| Re-lining founts | 26 |
| Running water at founts | 24 |
| Soda— | |
| " How to keep cool | 22–23 |
| " Trade | 5 |
| " Two kinds of | 17 |
| Still drinks | 15–149 |
| How to make | 16 |
| Orange and others | 141 |
| Sour drinks | 142 |
| Cranberry phosphate | 143 |
| Lemon " | 145 |
| Lactart " (Saxe's) | 146 |
| Orange phosphate | 127 |
| Pineapple " | 148 |
| Vichy " | 149 |
| Wild cherry phosphate | 141½ |
| Syrups, simple | 29 |
| Ambrosia | 33 |
| Banana | 34 |
| Base of flavored | 28 |
| Chocolate No. 1 (Saxe's) | 35 |
| " No. 2 " | 36 |
| " Yabara | 37 |
| Coca-phosphates | 95 |

**Simple Syrups.**—*Continued.*

|  | NO. |
|---|---|
| Coffee | 38 |
| Cranberry | 144 |
| Currant, red | 39 |
| Crabapple cider | 41 |
| Cream | 43 |
| Diamond | 42 |
| Don't Care | 44 |
| Ginger | 45 |
| " Canton | 40 |
| " fruit | 48 |
| " fizz | 49 |
| Hock or claret | 50 |
| Honey dew | 51 |
| Klub soda | 53 |
| Lemon (Saxe's) | 54 |
| " sherbet | 56 |
| Mountain dew | 57 |
| " pink | 58 |
| Nectar No. 1 | 64 |
| " No. 2 | 65 |
| Nectarine | 66 |
| Orgeat | 67 |
| Orange | 68 |
| " sherbet | 70 |
| " (blood) phosphate | 71 |
| Opera bouquet | 72 |
| Pineapple No. 1 | 73 |
| " No. 2 | 74 |
| Punchine | 121 |

# INDEX.

| Simple Syrups.—*Continued.* | NO. |
|---|---|
| Raspberry No. 1 | 75 |
| " No. 2 | 76 |
| Razzle dazzle | 77 |
| Sarsaparilla | 85 |
| " Mexican | 59 |
| Strawberry No. 1 | 79 |
| " No. 2 | 80 |
| Swizzle fizz | 81 |
| Solferino | 82 |
| Sherbet No. 1 | 83 |
| " No. 2 | 84 |
| Vanilla | 87 |
| " cream | 88 |
| Tinct. curcuma | 55 |
| Tonic drinks | 152 |
| Syrups, concentrated— | |
| Strawberry | 160 |
| Wild grape | 89 |
| Pineapple | 161 |

INDEX.

## SAXE'S NEW DRINKS FOR 1894.

| | PAGE. |
|---|---|
| Appleade | 98 |
| April Blossoms | 94 |
| August Vitalizer | 95 |
| Cherry Orange Phosphate | 97 |
| Gingerade | 98 |
| July Bracer | 95 |
| June Tonic | 95 |
| Louisville Punch | 97 |
| May Bells | 94 |
| New Orleans Punch | 97 |
| Nectine | 98 |
| October Favorite | 96 |
| Orangena | 99 |
| September Blessing | 96 |

## SAXE'S FORMULAS FOR HOT DRINKS.

| | |
|---|---|
| Articles necessary for operating a Hot Soda Water Apparatus | 102 |
| Instructions | 101-3 |
| Hot Chocolate | 104 |
| Hot Lemon | 105 |
| Hot Ginger Syrup | 105 |
| Hot Clam Broth | 106 |
| Hot Clam Juice and Lemon | 106 |
| Hot Beef Tea | 106 |
| Hot Beef and Celery | 106 |
| Hot Oyster Juice | 107 |
| Hot Egg Phosphate | 107 |
| Hot Egg Lemonade | 107 |
| Hot Egg Punch | 108 |
| Hot Lime Juice Flip | 108 |
| Hot Malted Milk | 109 |
| Hot Nervine | 109 |
| Manitoba Punch | 108 |
| Saxe's Concentrated Coffee Extract | 103 |
| To Serve Hot Coffee | 104 |
| Whipped Cream | 103 |
| Formula for cleaning Ice Cream Soda Glasses | 110 |

**WHEN** Attractive Designs, Purity of Beverages, Durability of Construction, Convenience of Operation, Cleanliness, Economy in the Use of Ice, and the most intense degree of coldness

## CEASE TO BE IMPORTANT

in the Construction of Soda Water Apparatus,

**THEN** Puffer's Frigid Soda Apparatus MAY

*cease to lead all competitors*

### BUT NOT UNTIL THEN.

Viewed by experts in the light of modern requirements,

**PUFFER'S FRIGID APPARATUS**

is the best apparatus manufactured.

SEND FOR FULL ILLUSTRATED CATALOGUE.

Milton Keynes UK
Ingram Content Group UK Ltd.
UKHW021309030424
440557UK00001B/143